a short &happy guide to
Civics

Deborah Cupples
University of Florida Levin College of Law

A SHORT & HAPPY GUIDE® SERIES

WEST
ACADEMIC
PUBLISHING

a short & happy guide series is a trademark registered in the U.S. Patent and Trademark Office.

Printed in the United States of America

ISBN: 978-1-64708-215-4

This book is dedicated to a couple who spent decades applying their knowledge of civics and law to protecting other people's rights:

Prof. Fletcher Baldwin (January 5, 1933-February 18, 2020)

and

Dr. Nancy Toman Baldwin

Acknowledgments

Many thanks to the following people for helping me with the editorial or publishing process:

- Victorina Basauri
- Susan Carr
- Pam Chandler
- Christina Coronado
- Jared Coronado
- Cami Cupples
- Jon Harkness
- Louis Higgins
- James Kirkpatrick
- Catherine Kai Lewis
- Carol Logie
- Carl J. Olsen
- Rod Olson
- Bill Reynolds
- Melissa Rider
- Laura Rosenbury
- Kendra Siler-Marsiglio
- Theresa Reid
- Margaret Temple-Smith
- Diane Tomlinson
- Kerry Travilla-Bown
- Sylvia Ward Schultz

What You Will Get from This Book

The law comes from governments and affects almost everything we do in business, at our jobs, and in our personal lives. It's unavoidable.

Civics is the study of (1) citizens' rights and duties and (2) government's structures and functions. A civics background is useful—

- If you study law or work in the legal profession.

- If you work in government or politics.

- If you work in a government-regulated industry.

- If you just want to be better informed.

Through no fault of their own, many people didn't get an adequate civics background in high school or college. Results from an American Bar Association survey confirm that civics education among members of the public is lacking.[1]

One result is that many people have trouble sorting out facts from fiction that they find on the Internet and other media. People who don't have a civics background are at a disadvantage compared to people who do have it.

Whatever your reason for wanting to improve your civics knowledge, this book can help you "get up to speed" on the basics—and pretty quickly.

You can also follow directions printed inside the cover of this book to take online quizzes to test yourself on what you've learned. These quizzes are designed as a learning tool.

---

[1] American Bar Association, *ABA Survey of Civic Literacy* (2019), https://www.americanbar.org/content/dam/aba/images/news/2019/05/ABASurveyOfCivicLiteracy.pdf.

Sources & Citations

Within chapter paragraphs, references to the **U.S. Constitution** are shorthanded, for example—

- Article II.

- Article I, Section 3.

- 25th Amendment.

Federal statutes, which are in the United States Code, are also shorthanded:

- U.S. Code, Title 5.

- 5 U.S. Code § 21 (meaning Title 5, section 21).

References to other parts of the book follow this format:

- This book, chapter 2.

- Chapter 2.

- Appendix 1.

A copy of the U.S. Constitution is in Appendix 1, toward the end of this book. A copy of the Declaration of Independence is in Appendix 2.

The citations in this book *do not follow the Bluebook* or any other prescribed format.

Table of Contents

A Short & Happy Guide to Civics

CHAPTER 1

Basic Concepts of American Law & Government

Rule of Law Versus "Rule of Men"

Under **the Rule of Law**, no one is above the law: not private individuals, not government officials—not even the U.S. President.

The Rule of Law protects people's rights partly by defining governments' powers and limits. The idea is to prevent the arbitrary use of power so that laws are enforced similarly for all people, which promotes fairness and predictability.

Under the "Rule of Men" (or women or people), the people in charge decide what the law is and how it's enforced, making things about as predictable as a Las Vegas slot machine. Under that system, a ruler's buddy who stole $5 million might get away with it, while an ordinary person who stole a sandwich might do jail time.

The first use of the phrase "Rule of Law" is unclear, but it's not a new concept. Over 2,000 years ago, Aristotle argued: "It is more proper that **the law should govern** than any one of its citizens."

Fast forward to 1776, when Thomas Paine (one of America's Founding Fathers) published a pamphlet called *Common Sense*, intended to persuade the colonies to declare independence from Britain. Paine wrote,

> "For as in absolute governments the King is law, so **in free countries the law ought to be King**; and there ought to be no other."

America's Founding Fathers set up our nation under the Rule of Law because they didn't like tyranny. They didn't want to live under a king's—or any dictator's—arbitrary or unfair use of power.

The Founding Fathers made that clear in the *Declaration of Independence*, where they bluntly listed reasons for declaring independence from Britain, including the King's failures, cruelty, and abuses of power.

The *Declaration of Independence* is in Appendix 2 of this book. It's a fairly quick read, a lot shorter than the Constitution.

Levels of Government in the U.S.

In the United States, there are 3 basic levels of government:

(1) The U.S. (federal) Government.

(2) The 50 states' governments.

(3) Local governments, like counties or cities.

Also, some Native American tribes have some self-governance powers, as do U.S. territories like Puerto Rico.

Basic Concepts: U.S. (Federal) Government

Structure and Functions

The federal government has 3 branches:

(1) Legislative Branch (Congress).

(2) Executive Branch (President).

(3) Judicial Branch (Courts).

They are **co-equal branches**, meaning no branch ranks higher than another.

The government's power is divided among the 3 branches. Congress legislates (makes laws). The Executive Branch executes and enforces laws. The Judicial Branch interprets laws. Think of it this way:

- Congress sets policies.

- The executive branch puts the policies into effect.

- The courts play referee, deciding whether government action complies with the law.

There's a lot more to it, which is why each branch has its own chapter in this book (Chapters 2, 3, and 4).

Separation of Powers & Checks and Balances

Separation of Powers is a crucial concept in American government: it prohibits one branch of government from exercising another branch's powers. Congress doesn't enforce laws, and the President doesn't decide court cases.

The Constitution created a system of **checks and balances** partly by—

- Separating the branches' powers.

- Requiring the branches to cooperate to use some shared powers.

The Constitution pits the branches against each other, so each branch acts as a check on (restrains) the other branches.

Push, pull, bargain, fight. It can be intense—when government is working the way it should.

Then there's the cooperation element. Even within Congress, some power is shared. Congress is **bicameral**—meaning divided into 2 houses, also called **chambers**:

(1) The House of Representatives.

(2) The Senate.

For Congress to pass a law, for example, both chambers must approve it through a majority vote in each chamber. It sounds easier than it usually is (more in Chapter 3).

Lawmaking is an example of checks and balances at work. Let's say that Congress passes a **bill** (a proposed law). If the President signs the bill, it becomes an actual law.

But the President could **veto** (reject) the bill. The President's veto acts as a *check* against Congress's power.

If the President vetoes the bill, Congress could **override the veto,** and the bill would become law without the President's approval. By overriding a veto, Congress acts as a *check* against the President's power.

Even if the bill becomes law, a court could eventually strike it down as unconstitutional. By doing that, the Judicial Branch would act as a *check* against the other two branches' powers.

Why such a complex system? Because the Framers of the Constitution wanted to prevent tyranny by not placing too much power in any one set of hands.

Types of Laws & Related Concepts

Overview

In the U.S., there are 5 major types of laws:

- Constitutions.

- Statutes.

- Regulations.

- Local-government ordinances.

- Case law.

They are covered in the rest of this chapter.

U.S. Constitution: Supreme Law of the Land

Structure and Basic Functions

The U.S. Constitution is the **supreme law of the land**, as stated in the **Supremacy Clause** of the Constitution (Article VI). Any federal, state, or local law that violates the Constitution is unconstitutional (invalid)—after a court says so.

The **Framers of the Constitution** were the people who attended the Constitutional Convention in 1787 or helped write the document. For history, check the National Archives (www.archives. gov).

The Constitution is a starting point for governments' powers and people's rights. Basically, here's what the Constitution does:

- Creates the federal government's 3 branches.

- Assigns powers to the branches.

- Addresses the relationship between the federal and state governments.

- Addresses relations between the states.

- Grants rights to people.

Below is a basic outline of what the Constitution covers.

Outline of Constitution

- **Article I**: Legislative Branch (Congress)
- **Article II**: Executive Branch (President)
- **Article III**: Judicial Branch (Courts)
- **Article IV**: State Related Issues
- **Article V**: How to Amend the Constitution
- **Article VI**: Constitution and U.S. law are Supreme; oaths of office; no religious tests for people qualifying for office
- **Article VII**: Ratification of the Constitution
- **Amendments** (including *Bill of Rights*)

The Constitution's text is in Appendix 1 of this book.

The Constitution Isn't Crystal Clear

Parts of the Constitution aren't clear, so we can't always discover the legal impact from the literal meaning of the words on the page. That's one reason for lawsuits about the Constitution's meaning. Interpreting the Constitution is part of our courts' job (more in Chapter 4).

Parts of the Constitution lack details because it wasn't meant to micromanage everything. It contains some details, but **mostly the Constitution states broad principles** and leaves the rest for the 3 branches to hammer out.

Partly because of its broad nature, the Constitution still applies 200+ years after it was written. For example, airplanes didn't exist when the Constitution was written, but Congress's powers were phrased broadly enough to enable Congress to pass laws about air travel.

The Amendments & People's Rights

Basic Overview

So far, there are only 27 amendments to the Constitution. The **Bill of Rights** refers to the first 10 amendments, which were **ratified** (adopted) in 1791. The first 9 amendments cover rights directly granted to individuals. Below is a list of topics that the Bill of Rights covers:

- **1st:** Freedom of religion, speech, press, and assembly; right to petition government.

- **2nd:** Right to be armed (weapons).

- **3rd:** Right to stop soldiers from taking over people's homes in peacetime.

- **4th:** Protection against unreasonable searches and seizures.

- **5th:** Rights and protections regarding criminal charges and government's taking of life, liberty, and property.

- **6th:** Rights regarding criminal trials.

- **7th:** Rights regarding jury trials in civil cases.

- **8th:** Protections regarding bail, fines, and cruel and unusual punishment.

- **9th:** Statement that the people have more rights than those listed in the Constitution.

- **10th:** The states' power to pass laws.

Only 17 other amendments have been ratified (from 1795-1992). Below are the amendments ratified after the Bill of Rights *that focus on individual rights or freedoms*:

- **13th:** Abolition of slavery.
- **14th:** Protection of people's Constitutional rights *in the states* and equal protection under the law, among other things.
- **15th:** Right to vote regardless of person's race.
- **18th:** Prohibition of alcohol in the U.S.
- **19th:** Right to vote regardless of person's sex.
- **21st:** Repeal of 18th Amendment: alcohol was legal again.
- **24th:** Prohibition of poll taxes (charging people money to vote).
- **26th:** Right to vote at age 18 (it had been 21).

People have more rights than are listed in the Constitution (9th Amendment). Courts' interpretations of the Constitution affect the nature of our rights.

For example, the Constitution doesn't mention the Internet—it didn't exist when the Constitution was written. In the 1990s, the U.S. Supreme Court decided that 1st Amendment free-speech rights apply to things people publish on the Internet.

The word "privacy" isn't in the Constitution, but the Supreme Court decided that certain parts of the Constitution give us the right of privacy. Other rights grew out of the right of privacy, like the right to use birth control—which was not fully legalized throughout the U.S. until the 1972 U.S. Supreme Court case *Eisenstadt v. Baird*.

Constitutional rights are **not absolute**. We have free-speech rights, for example, but governments can sometimes restrict the **time, place, and manner** in which we exercise those rights. For example, the police can escort someone out of a city council meeting for disrupting the event by shouting insults.

The 2nd Amendment is another example. It gives us a right to have guns. But governments can, for example, restrict us from bringing guns into a courthouse or other government building.

Mostly, the amendments that grant individual rights protect people against **government action**, not private citizens' action. So, you wouldn't violate the 1st Amendment by stopping a drunk guest from giving a speech at your birthday party.

Only U.S. citizens have the right to vote, but the Bill of Rights **protects citizens *and* non-citizens** within the U.S. For example, if a tourist from Britain commits a crime in and is prosecuted in the U.S., that person would have 5th Amendment rights.

U.S. Territories, Washington D.C., & Citizenship

A U.S. territory is a geographical area (1) that is not a U.S. state and (2) that is under the U.S. Government's authority yet somewhat self-governed. The 5 major U.S. territories are listed alphabetically—

- American Samoa.
- Guam.
- Northern Mariana Islands.
- Puerto Rico.
- U.S. Virgin Islands.

U.S. citizenship is granted to people **born in** 4 of the territories: Guam, the Northern Mariana Islands, Puerto Rico, and the U.S. Virgin Islands.

As citizens, they can vote for delegates to the U.S. House (more in Chapter 2). They can't vote for U.S. senators because only *states* have U.S. senators (Article I, Section 3).

U.S. citizens who are also citizens of a territory can't vote for U.S. presidents because the Constitution (Article II, Section 1) allows *only states* to participate in the electoral college (more in Chapter 3).

American Samoa doesn't have **birthright citizenship**, so being born there doesn't guarantee U.S. citizenship to a person.

Congress could change citizenship policies for any U.S. territory because the Constitution gives Congress the power to create and manage the territories (Article IV, Section 3).

The Amendments & Governmental Functions

Below are examples of amendments that deal directly with *governmental functions*:

- **11th:** Limits courts' jurisdiction in some lawsuits against states.

- **12th:** Changes how presidents are elected.

- **16th:** Gives Congress power to impose income tax.

- **17th:** Allows the people (instead of the states) to elect senators.

- **20th:** Sets dates when a president's and Congress's terms end; discusses presidential vacancy.

- **22nd:** Sets term limits for presidents.

- **23rd:** Gives Washington, D.C. electors in the Electoral College (presidential elections).

- **25th:** Creates ways to remove a president from office other than impeachment.

- **27th:** Limits pay raises for members of Congress.

Details about the powers and functions of the U.S. Government's branches are in Chapters 2, 3, and 4. The full text of the Constitution is in Appendix 1. It's worth looking at.

States' Relations & "Full Faith and Credit"

The Constitution's **full faith and credit clause** states, "Full Faith and Credit shall be given in each State to the public Acts, Records, and judicial Proceedings of every other State." (Article IV, Section 1). The U.S. Supreme Court said this about the clause:

> The Full Faith and Credit Clause is one of several provisions in the Federal Constitution designed to transform the several States from independent sovereignties into a single, unified Nation.[1]

That makes sense. If states didn't give full faith and credit, each state would be like a separate nation, making it difficult for citizens of one state to travel or move to another state.

The clause doesn't force one state to adopt another state's laws. For example, marijuana is legal in Colorado, but it's *illegal* for anyone—even a Colorado citizen—to smoke weed in a state where it's illegal.

The clause typically applies to courts' judgments relating to many family law issues. For example, if parents lawfully adopt a child in Georgia, then Alabama would have to recognize the adoption.[2] If that weren't so, people might have to re-adopt their kids when moving to another state. States also typically give full faith and credit to court judgments relating to lawful marriages and divorces that occurred in other states.

People in court have tried using the full faith and credit clause in many types of cases, including contracts, corporate law, insurance claims, criminal, personal injury. . . . Some have succeeded, and some haven't.[3]

---

[1] *Allstate Ins. Co. v. Hague*, 449 U.S. 302, 322 (1981).

[2] *V.L. v. E.L.*, 136 S. Ct. 1017, 1020 (2016).

[3] 16B Am. Jur. 2d Constitutional Law § 1029.

The question of whether the clause applies in a case can be very complex. The rulings of federal and state courts may come into play, as well as federal and state statutes.

Amending the U.S. Constitution Isn't Easy

Amending (changing) the U.S. Constitution isn't easy (Article V). A *proposed* amendment can come from 2 sources:

(1)   The U.S. Congress.

(2)   The states.

After an amendment is proposed, it's up to the states to **ratify** it (make it valid). Ratification requires approval from 3/4 of the states' legislatures or of the states at a convention.

That means *thousands* of legislators would be involved in amending the Constitution. It's not easy to get so many people to agree on every word of an amendment.

State Constitutions

Like the U.S. Constitution, state constitutions typically address government powers and people's rights and freedoms. State constitutions can give people greater rights than the U.S. Constitution *but not lesser rights*. For example, Florida's Constitution grants people the right to use medical marijuana, but the U.S. Constitution doesn't (future legal battles might change some states' marijuana laws).

When it comes to people's rights, think of the U.S. Constitution as the floor. A state constitution can build upon the floor but can't go below it.

Different states have different processes for amending the state's constitution. You can find your state's constitution by searching online for "constitution" + your state.

Statutes

Federal Statutes

A **statute** is a law passed by a legislative (lawmaking) body. **Congress** is the U.S. Government's legislative body. Congress passes federal statutes, usually with the President's approval (more about Congress in Chapter 2).

The word **legislation** can refer to different things, like federal statutes, state statutes, and local government ordinances.

Statutes can give us rights or privileges. For example, statutes give authors certain rights over the books they write. Statutes entitle some people to social security benefits.

Statutes can impose duties, like paying taxes. Statutes can also affect the power and duties of governments. For example, the Constitution established the U.S. Supreme Court but gave Congress the power to create lower federal courts (more in Chapter 4). Congress created lower courts through statutes.

Congress can pass statutes about many things, as long as (1) the statute doesn't violate the Constitution and (2) Congress doesn't exceed its constitutional authority. Chapter 2 covers more about Congress's authority.

Federal statutes are in the **U.S. Code**, which is huge. It's divided into numbered **titles** that cover different topics, for example—

- Title 2: Congress.

- Title 18: Crimes.

- Title 26: Internal Revenue Code.

- Title 52: Voting and elections.

You can find the U.S. Code online at multiple sites, including the U.S. House of Representatives (https://uscode.house.gov) and the Legal Information Institute (www.law.cornell.edu/uscode).

State Statutes and Legislatures

A state's statutes are passed by the state's legislative body, usually with the governor's approval. Most states call their legislative body the "legislature." Some states, like Colorado and Illinois, call it "The General Assembly." The legislatures in New Hampshire and Massachusetts are called "The General Court" (confusing but *not a typo*).

Most states have a **bicameral** legislature: made up of two chambers, like the U.S. Congress (more about Congress in Chapter 2). Nebraska is the only state that has a **unicameral** legislature— only one chamber.

This book refers to any state's legislative body as a *legislature*. To find your state's legislature online, search for "legislature" + your state.

Some state statutes apply to all people in the state, even non-residents. For example, a non-resident who commits theft while visiting Iowa could be arrested for it in that state. Some states' statutes apply to only residents, like voter-registration statutes.

State governments can't regulate by statute (or otherwise) anything that's reserved for the federal government. Copyright law, for example, is reserved for the federal government.

But state governments can regulate things that aren't reserved for the federal government (per the 10th Amendment). For example, state laws deal with drivers' licenses, marriage, and wills. State governments regulate many professions, like the medical profession.

Police Power is a constitutional-law concept referring to each state's right to exercise power to promote the public's health, safety, morals, or welfare within that state. Passing statutes is one way for states to exercise their police power.

Different states handle issues differently through statutes. For example, California and Colorado handle divorce differently. Texas has different laws than Florida against texting while driving.

States have different names for their collection of statutes, like the *Idaho Statutes*, the *California Code*, and the *General Laws of Massachusetts*. To find your state's statutes, search online for "statutes" + your state.

To be valid, a state statute can't violate the U.S. Constitution, other U.S. laws, or that state's constitution.

Regulations (Rules)

Federal Agencies & Regulations

Administrative agencies are government entities that execute or enforce laws and policies. The U.S. Treasury Department and the U.S. Department of Education are examples of administrative agencies (more in Chapter 3).

Federal **regulations** are rules that are **promulgated** (adopted) by an administrative agency. The words "regulations" and "rules" are often used interchangeably. In the rest of this section, "rule" is used.

Some rules address an agency's internal operations. Some regulate the conduct of people, businesses or other entities. For example, the Federal Trade Commission has rules against businesses using false advertising. Congress passed statutes requiring most U.S. citizens to have passports before leaving the U.S., and the U.S. State Department made rules for how citizens get a passport.

Administrative Law is about administrative agencies' regulations and procedures. It's complex and includes procedures and other requirements for rulemaking.

Within constitutional limits, Congress can give an administrative agency broad or specific rulemaking authority. For example, Congress could direct the Department of Transportation (DOT) to set safety standards for cars and leave some details to the DOT—or Congress could be more detailed and direct the DOT to require airbags in cars.

The Constitution trumps rules, as it trumps all laws. Statutes trump rules because statutes give administrative agencies the power to make rules. What Congress gives by statute, Congress can take away or change by statute.

Federal administrative agencies' rules are in the **Code of Federal Regulations**. Many types of rules must be published in the **Federal Register**, which is the "daily journal" of the U.S. Government (www.federalregister.gov). The rule-publishing requirement promotes the Rule of Law by—

(1) Holding agencies accountable for following proper procedures and

(2) Giving people notice of the rules that affect them.

State Agencies & Regulations

States have administrative agencies that adopt rules. States also have their own body of administrative law. To be valid, a state agency's rules must not violate the U.S. Constitution, U.S. statutes, the state's constitution, or the state's statutes.

Typically, a state's collection of rules is called a **Code**, like the *Wisconsin Administrative Code* and the *Missouri Code of State Regulations*. To find your state's rules online, search for "regulations" + your state.

Local Government Ordinances

Ordinances are laws passed by a local government's legislative body, like a County Commission, County Council, City Commission, City Council, etc. Two states have different names for what most states call "counties": Alaska calls them "boroughs," and Louisiana calls them "parishes."

Ordinances can protect rights. For example, more than 100 cities and counties have ordinances that prohibit employers from practicing employment discrimination based on gender identity.

Ordinances can also impose duties. An ordinance might limit how you can use land in an area of a city or how late at night you can buy beer.

Local governments' powers come from their state's law (including the state's constitution). To be valid, ordinances can't violate federal law or the relevant state's law.

To find your local ordinances online, search for "ordinances" + your city or county + your state. Another source is **Municode** (www.municode.com), which is handy for legal research.

Case Law (and Related Concepts)

Let's start with some case-law-related concepts. A **lawsuit** is a legal action brought in court by a party who is accusing another party of not fulfilling a legal duty. Other words for a lawsuit include *suit*, *action*, and *case*.

In a **criminal case**, a government entity empowered to prosecute crimes brings the case (1) to accuse a defendant of committing a crime and (2) to punish the defendant—usually through fines or jail time.

For now, think of a **civil case** as simply non-criminal: as not involving a crime (more in Chapter 4).

If a court decides a case, either criminal or civil, the court might render an **opinion**: a written explanation of the court's decision in the case. Typically, a court's opinion explains—

(1)   The facts and legal issues involved in a case,

(2)   The court's **holding** (a ruling about how the law applies to the facts in that case), and

(3)   The reasoning behind the holding.

"Case" can also refer to a specific court opinion (as in, *the lawyer read a U.S. Supreme Court case about copyrights*).

Warning: legal lingo can be confusing because multiple terms might refer to one concept, or one term might refer to multiple concepts.

Stare Decisis is a legal doctrine under which courts tend to stand by precedents. **Precedent** can refer to a *past* court opinion or to a court's ruling in a *past* case.

The idea is that courts should follow relevant precedents: i.e., rule the same way in a present case as in a past case involving the same facts and legal issues. By following precedents, courts promote predictability, fairness, and the Rule of Law.

Here's an example of how a court might set a precedent. Let's say that a new state statute imposes a 5-year prison sentence on anyone who "uses a gun" while committing robbery but only 3 years if the robber doesn't use a gun.

Annie The Armed Robber had a gun in her backpack while robbing Victor. She didn't threaten him with the gun. She didn't even take it out of her backpack. At trial, the prosecutor argues that Annie should go to prison for 5 years because she *had* the gun and could have used it. Annie's lawyer argues that Annie should get 3 years because she didn't actually use the gun.

In that case, the court would answer a legal question like this: *Does the statute's 5-year sentence apply if a robber had a gun but did not use it during the robbery?*

The court's answer would set a precedent for how other courts should interpret and apply that statute. That precedent would become part of the body of case law in that court's jurisdiction (more about jurisdiction in Chapter 4).

Finally, we get to **case law**, which the U.S. Court system's website explains this way:

> The law as established in previous court decisions. A synonym for legal precedent.

Put another way, "case law" refers to legal principles stated in courts' opinions. Both federal and state courts create case law.

Case law can address many types of legal questions, like how to interpret a statute, whether a statute is constitutional, or whether a government official's actions are lawful.

Case law can cover situations that statutes don't. Let's say that your state doesn't have a statute relating to what happens if your neighbor's tree falls and crushes your car. If you sue, a court might decide—based on case law—that your neighbor owes you money to replace your car.

Case law is crucial to the Rule of Law. Without case law, judges could decide cases based on personal feelings or absurd reasons, which would create uncertainty and unfairness.

Common law refers to a legal system that relies on case law— that is, on principles stated in precedents (past court cases). The common law system began in England and is in use in the U.S.

"Common law" can also refer to the collection of legal principles found in case law. Because each state has a separate legal system, different states have different bodies of common law and case law. Louisiana's legal system is different from most other states' because it arose from the Napoleonic Code (instead of English common law).

While it can affect public policy, case law isn't always the final word. If Congress or a state legislature doesn't like a court's interpretation of a statute, for example, Congress or that legislature could change the statute to get a different outcome (more in Chapter 4).

CHAPTER 2

Legislative Branch: Congress & Its Agencies

Congress's Structure & Key Lingo

Congress has two chambers, also called "**houses**":

- The U.S. House of Representatives (lower chamber).

- The U.S. Senate (upper chamber).

"The House" is shorthand for the House of Representatives. The Senate is called "The Senate."

The **Senate** has **100** members, called "senators." Each state has two senators. Because each state has an equal number of senators, small states have the same voting power as large states in the Senate.

The **House** has **435** full-voting members. The bigger a state's population, the more representatives the state has in the House. Thus, higher-population states have more voting power in the House.

The House also has 6 so-called "non-voting" delegates:

- The Resident Commissioner of Puerto Rico.

- 1 delegate from Washington, D.C.

- 4 delegates, one each for American Samoa; Guam; the Northern Mariana Islands; and the U.S. Virgin Islands.

D.C. isn't a "territory," but the other areas are (this book, chapter 2).

"Non-voting" delegates to the House can serve on and vote in many committees. They have most other privileges that House members have.[1]

"Non-voting" members *can't* vote on the House floor to pass a bill and face other voting limits. The limits stem from the word "Member" in the Constitution: House *members* represent *states* and have legislative power, but Washington, D.C. and the territories aren't states (Article I, Section 2).[2]

Typically, senators are addressed as Senator + last name (Senator Adams). For House Members, you have options:

- Representative + last name.

- Congressman + last name.

- Congresswoman + last name.

News media often refer to members in writing by last name + party + state:

- House Member: Rep. Adams (R-NY).

- Senator: Sen. Adams (D-TX).

For **independents**, news media use the letter "I": for example, Sen. Sanders (I-VT).

---

[1]   *Rules of the U.S. House of Representatives*, Rules I-V (116th Congress).

[2]   *Michel v. Anderson*, 817 F. Supp. 126, 134 (D.D.C. 1993), aff'd, 14 F.3d 623 (D.C. Cir. 1994).

Congress's Powers & Duties

Legislative Powers

Through its legislative powers, Congress typically does three things:

- Sets public policy.
- Appropriates funds (decides how tax dollars are spent).
- Guides the execution of policies and enforcement of laws.

Those things are intertwined. It costs money to execute policies and enforce laws. Public policy and laws mean little if they aren't executed or enforced.

Through legislation, Congress has guided the execution of policy and enforcement of laws by (1) creating agencies to do the executing and enforcing and (2) delegating some tasks to existing agencies.

Public policy is a broad term. Congress sets public policy relating to many issues: for example, healthcare, taxes, education, housing, the environment. . . .

Among other things, Congress can **legislate** (make laws) about the items listed in Article 1, Section 8 of the Constitution, which are called the **enumerated powers**. More than 20 items are listed, and here are a few examples:

- Power to provide for the common defense and general welfare of the U.S.
- Power to raise revenue.
- Power to set up post offices.
- Power to set immigration law.
- Power to declare war.

Some enumerated powers are more clearly written than others. Some are very broad, depending on how courts choose to interpret them (more in Chapter 4).

There *are* limits on what Congress is authorized to regulate, but what are they? That question has fueled lawsuits as intense as the action on a hockey rink.

Some court cases over Congress's authority focus on Congress's actions **within the federal government arena**. That type of case addresses whether Congress exercised powers that belong to a different branch of the U.S. Government (executive or judicial branch).[3]

Some cases are about whether Congress had infringed on a **state's right** of self-government. Often, Congress's power is at odds with the states' rights to regulate things within their borders. It can be fierce.

Why? Because there's a lot at stake for a lot of people. If Congress can regulate certain activities, the states lose power. Also, complying with federal law can cost money for states, businesses, or people.

For example, the U.S. government started heavily regulating air-polluting businesses in the 1970s partly because some states allowed industries to cause more pollution than other states. Here are some basic arguments:

- **State:** I have rights! The U.S. government is violating those rights by regulating pollution within *my* borders.

- **Business:** Complying with anti-pollution laws costs me money and drives up the price of my products, so the U.S. government should stop regulating pollution.

---

[3]   See *I.N.S. v. Chadha*, 462 U.S. 919 (1983) (encroachment on executive branch); *Ex parte McCardle*, 74 U.S. 506 (1868) (encroachment on judiciary).

- **U.S. Gov.:** Pollution won't stay in one state. *Not regulating* polluting industries will damage the environment, harm people's health, and cost money in the long run.

The arguments are more complex than that, but the point is that many interests are affected by the answer to this question: *How far do Congress's powers reach?*

Oversight: Power & Duty

As part of our system of checks and balances, Congress has the power and duty to exercise **oversight**—to check on whether government officials are doing what they're supposed to. One part of the oversight powers is the power to remove government officials from office (more in the next subsection).

Many people think of *congressional oversight* as applying to only the Executive Branch. That may be because the executive branch is bigger than the other two branches. It's more involved in the government's day-to-day operations, so there's more to oversee and more that can go wrong.

But Congress also has some oversight power relating to the Judicial Branch, evident in Congress's power to remove judges from federal courts. That and Congress, through legislation, establishes and funds the nation's lower courts.

As well as a power, Congressional oversight is a **duty to the people** who elect members of Congress. Oversight boils down to holding government officials accountable for—

- Spending tax dollars appropriately and

- Otherwise fulfilling their duties.

Oversight powers and duties relate partly to Congress's appropriation power. To know whether government officials are spending tax dollars the way that Congress had directed them to, Congress must exercise oversight.

It's not only about money. Congress must exercise oversight also to know whether government officials are properly executing policy and enforcing laws.

Typically, Congress exercises oversight through Committees (more about committees in chapter 2). It's not always about officials misbehaving. Sometimes, oversight is routine. The oversight process might involve a committee's—

- Being briefed routinely by government officials.

- Holding special hearings to get witness testimony.

- Requesting and reviewing documents.

- Investigating someone or something.

Congressional oversight is affected by constitutional principles, laws that Congress has passed, and the rules of the House and Senate.

Powers Belonging to Congress Only

Removing Officials from Office

As part of the system's *checks and balances*, the **impeachment process** is one way for Congress to remove certain officials from office, including federal judges, cabinet members, and the President (Article I, Sections 2 & 3 and Article II, Section 4).

Impeachment, alone, *doesn't remove* an official from office. To **impeach** means only to accuse someone of wrongdoing. That's it. To remove an official from office requires that—

(1) a majority of the House votes to impeach (up to **218*** members);

(2) the Senate holds an impeachment trial, presided over by the Chief Justice of the U.S. Supreme Court; and

(3) a 2/3 majority of the Senate votes to convict (up to **67*** senators).

*A **majority** vote of the *members present* is required. If only 97 senators are present, a 2/3 majority would be **65** members. If only 431 House members are present, a majority would be **216**.

Removal from office is the only result of a conviction that stems from impeachment. There aren't other penalties, but impeachment doesn't stop law enforcement from prosecuting a removed official down the road for a crime.

Impeachment is rare. In more than 200 years (1789-2018), the House had *started* impeachment proceedings **less than 75 times**. Less than one-third of the proceedings led to full impeachments. **Only 8 officials**, all federal judges, were convicted by the Senate and removed from office (https://history.house.gov/).

Only two U.S. presidents have been impeached, but they weren't removed from office. Ways to remove a president, and there are more than one, are covered in Chapter 3. Removal of judges is covered in Chapter 4. Removal of members of Congress is covered in the next subsection.

Rules & Enforcement for Each Chamber

The House makes its own rules for how it operates, and the Senate makes its own rules (Article I, Section 5). Each chamber's rules cover many issues, including—

- Members' conduct.

- Debating.

- Voting.

- Committee assignments.

- Penalties for members who violate rules.

Members of Congress can be **expelled** (removed) from office (Article I, Section 5). The House can expel a House member through a 2/3 majority vote of the House. The Senate can expel a senator through a 2/3 majority vote of the Senate.

Power to Confirm Appointments, Treaties & Agreements

Among other things, the President has the power (1) to appoint many government officials and (2) to make treaties with foreign governments. But the President can't do all of it alone.

To be valid, a president's appointments and treaties require **Senate consent**, meaning "approval" (Article II, Section 2). The approval process is also called *Senate confirmation.*

When a president appoints or "nominates" someone for an official position, the nomination typically goes to the relevant Senate committee. For example, the Senate Judiciary Committee would handle a nomination for the Attorney General position.

The Senate committee could move the nomination straight to a Senate floor vote. The committee could hold hearings about the nomination and later move it to a floor vote (or not). If the Senate does nothing, the nomination would die.

If the President appoints a Vice President because the last one died or left office, the appointment would require House *and* Senate approval (25th Amendment). International trade agreements require both House and Senate approval because Congress regulates international trade (Article I, Section 8).

Political Parties: Control & Leadership

The Congresses & Party Control

The word "Congress" refers to two things—

(1)　the legislative body generally and

(2)　that body during a specific 2-year period between congressional elections.

The Congresses are numbered. The **1st Congress** started in 1789 and ended in 1791. Congress's membership changes every two years because congressional elections happen every two years.

The two major parties are the Democratic Party and the Republican Party. Those parties *aren't mentioned* in the Constitution. They didn't exist in the 1700s. Still, those parties play **major roles** in Congress.

Below is a list of 10 Congresses and which party controlled each chamber:

Congress	Years	House Control	Senate Control
107th	2001-03	Repub.	Repub.
108th	2003-05	Repub.	Repub.
109th	2005-07	Repub.	Repub.
110th	2007-09	Dem.	Dem.
111th	2009-11	Dem.	Dem.
112th	2011-13	Repub.	Dem.
113th	2013-15	Repub.	Dem.
114th	2015-17	Repub.	Repub.

| 115th | 2017-19 | Repub. | Repub. |
| 116th | 2019-21 | Dem. | Repub. |

Which party controls a chamber (or both) has a huge impact on things like—

- Who leads the House and Senate.

- Which legislation is passed.

- The degree of oversight that Congress exercises.

Tension has always existed between the parties because they want different things. During some periods of history, the parties have been more likely to give and take and compromise.

During other periods, one party or both have refused to compromise or work with the other party. In that case, not much gets done unless the same party controls the House and Senate—and the President is willing to work with Congress.

In Congress, a **caucus** is a group of members. The House's two largest caucuses are the major-party caucuses:

- The House Democratic Caucus.

- The House Republican Conference.

All House Democrats are members of the Democratic Caucus. All Republican House Members are members of the Republican Conference. The House's major-party caucuses' websites are at www.dems.gov and www.gop.gov.

In the Senate, the major-party caucuses are called—

- The Senate Republican Conference.

- The Senate Democratic Caucus.

Typically, senators and House members who *aren't* members of a major party "caucus with" (join) one of the major-party caucuses. The major-party caucuses' websites are www.republicans.senate.gov and www.democrats.senate.gov.

Leadership in the House (Article I, Section 2)

The House can choose (spelled "chuse" in the 1700s) its leaders and officers. The House's head honcho is the **Speaker of the House** (Speaker), addressed as *Madam Speaker* or *Mister Speaker*. The Speaker is elected by the whole House and is usually in the majority party.

The Speaker is among the highest ranking and most powerful people in government. Why?

First, the Speaker is #2 in the presidential *order of succession*, (a.k.a. *line of succession*), behind the Vice President.[4] If both a current president and vice president are unable at the same time to fulfill the duties of office (due to incapacity, death, or another reason), the Speaker would become the acting president.

Second, the Speaker represents, leads, and presides over the House. Typically, the Speaker deals with the President and the Senate leaders, as well as representing the whole House and the majority party.

Among other things, the Speaker plays a big role in—

- Setting the House's policy agenda (e.g., one speaker's agenda included healthcare).
- Setting or changing the House's daily agenda (e.g., deciding when bills come up for a vote).
- Deciding whether members can speak on the House floor.
- Assigning members to committees.

---

[4] 3 U.S. Code § 19.

The Speaker can't force members to vote a certain way, **but** crossing the Speaker could come back to bite members who need the Speaker's cooperation down the road. That's politics.

Third, without the Speaker's cooperation, there's a lot that the President or Congress can't get done. Strong Speakers use that reality as a bargaining chip.

The House has other leadership positions: for example, the Majority Leader and Minority Leader. At the start of each new Congress, each political party caucus elects its own leaders.

The Speaker usually delegates some duties to other leaders. You can find details about the Speaker at www.house.gov.

Leadership in the Senate (Article I, Section 3)

The Senate and the House are different. The Senate is smaller, and its standing rules and customs focus more on members' rights and power than the House's rules do.

The Senate has two "Floor Leaders":

(1)   the **Senate Majority Leader** (Majority Leader) and

(2)   the **Senate Minority Leader** (Minority Leader).

Each is elected by its own political party's members. The Floor Leaders aren't mentioned in the Constitution. The positions evolved over time.

The Majority Leader has the advantage of leading the party that has more votes in the Senate. The parties' goals often clash. But the two floor leaders tend to cooperate and negotiate to keep the Senate's business moving along.

Both the Majority Leader and Minority Leader deal directly with the U.S. President and House leadership. The Minority Leader speaks for the minority party. The Majority Leader speaks for the majority party and the Senate as an institution.

The Majority leader plays a part in assigning majority-party senators to committees. The Minority Leader does the same for minority-party senators. **Committees are crucial**, and they're covered in this chapter.

Due to custom and efficiency, members of the Senate allow the Majority Leader the power to decide whether a bill or other matter is voted on by the Senate. That's a lot of power.

The **U.S. Vice President** is automatically the **President of the Senate** (Article I, Section 3). As the Senate President, the U.S. Vice President can't vote in the Senate except to break a tie and can't speak in the Senate unless the members consent. The Senate President does little more in the Senate than preside over it—and not often.

The Constitution requires the Senate to elect a **President Pro Tempore**: a.k.a., President Pro Tem (*pro tempore* means "for the time"). The President Pro Tem—or his or her designee—presides over the Senate when the Senate President is absent (Article I, Section 3). The President Pro Tem can vote and can address the Senate because he or she *is* an elected member of the Senate.

The Senate President Pro Tem is #3 in the **presidential order of succession**, just after the House Speaker (more in Chapter 3). The Senate Majority and Minority Leaders *aren't* in the order of succession to the presidency.

CMOs

There is power in numbers because voting is the main way of getting things done in Congress. Thus, members of Congress might join groups called **Congressional Member Organizations** (CMOs), also called "caucuses."

CMOs are groups of members who have interests in common or want to get certain things done. The House and Senate have CMOs, but each chamber deals with CMOs differently. Examples include—

- Congressional Black Caucus (race related).

- House Aerospace Caucus.

- Senate Bipartisan Small Brewer's Caucus (beer).

- Senate Human Rights Caucus.

For more about CMOs, search the House or Senate website for "caucus" or "CMO."

Committees: How Things Get Done

What They Are

It's hard enough to get 20 people to focus and accomplish anything. That can be as true for adults as for first-graders.

It's harder when 100 senators or 435 House members are involved. That's why much of Congress's work is divided up and assigned to **committees**: formal groups of members that focus on certain issues.

Each committee has **jurisdiction**—authority to deal with certain issues and tasks. Some committees' jurisdictions overlap.

The House and Senate have their own committees, but each chamber's committees are named and organized somewhat differently. Here are a few examples of committees:

- House Appropriations Committee.

- House Oversight and Reform Committee.

- Senate Energy and Natural Resources Committee.

- Senate Foreign Relations Committee.

For more about committees, start at the House's or Senate's website, and look for a link to "committees."

Role in Congressional Oversight

Different committees have oversight jurisdiction over different aspects of government. For example, the Senate Intelligence Committee has jurisdiction over agencies in the "Intelligence Community," like the CIA and Justice Department. The Senate Intel Committee can oversee and investigate agencies under its jurisdiction and can require them to regularly brief the committee.

Committees in both the House and Senate have oversight duties. Similar committees in the House and Senate might conduct separate investigations into the same issues at the same time.

Role in Legislative (Lawmaking) Process

Committees are crucial to lawmaking because they can decide whether to kill or stall a bill. Committees affect what a bill looks like before it goes to a full vote. The legislative process is covered in this chapter.

Subcommittees and Their Sub-Issues

Many committees cover broad issues that encompass sub-issues. Dividing those committees into **subcommittees** divides a committee's workload and makes it easier to get things done.

For example, the *House Appropriations Committee* deals with **appropriations** (deciding how tax dollars are spent). That's a huge category because Congress appropriates funds for thousands of government functions and agencies—too many things for an undivided committee to handle.

The House Appropriations Committee has 12 sub-committees (116th Congress), including—

- Subcommittee on Commerce, Justice, Science, and Related Agencies.

- Subcommittee on Defense.

- Subcommittee on Labor, Health and Human Services, Education, and Related Agencies.

Many Senate committees also have subcommittees. You can learn about specific subcommittees by starting at a major committee's webpage at the House or Senate website and finding a "subcommittees" link.

Types of Committees

There are three basic types of committees:

- Standing Committees.

- Select (or Special) Committees.

- Joint Committees.

Standing committees continue from one Congress to the next. They are permanent because their tasks are ongoing, like the *House Foreign Affairs Committee* and the *Senate Armed Services Committee*. The nation regularly deals with foreign affairs and military issues.

Select (or Special) committees handle special functions that are beyond a standing committee's capacity. Some select committees are permanent, like the Senate's *Select Committee on Ethics*. Some select committees are temporary, like the House select committee established to investigate terrorist attacks on U.S. facilities in Benghazi, Libya.

Joint committees have members from the House and the Senate. They handle issues or tasks of interest to both chambers. For example, the *Joint Committee on the Library* deals with the Library of Congress, which houses Congress's records.

Legislative (Lawmaking) Process

Basic Overview

Knowing basics about the legislative process can be helpful to people doing legal research—lawyers, judges, journalists. . . .

Bills are proposed laws. A bill can't become law unless the House and Senate pass **identical** versions of the bill.

Only a member of the House or Senate can introduce bills in that chamber. Members may introduce bills at the request of the President or other people, including lobbyists.

Most types of bills may originate in either chamber. But the Constitution requires that bills for raising revenue originate in the House (Article I, Section 7).

House bills originate in the House, and **Senate bills** originate in the Senate. Bills are labeled with an abbreviation + a number:

- H.R. 107 (House bills).

- S. 107 (Senate bills).

Different bills go through different processes before becoming laws. A simple illustration of the process is below.

Simple Illustration of House Bill That Becomes Law

- House member (sponsor) introduces bill:
    - Gives it to the Clerk of the House
      or
    - Puts it in the "hopper" (a box on the House floor).
- Clerk of the House assigns a number to the Bill.
- Bill is referred to House committee that has jurisdiction over bill's subject.

- Committee sends bill to the floor for consideration (for the whole House to consider and debate).

- House passes bill by majority vote on the floor.

- Senate passes identical version of bill.

- President signs bill-it becomes law.

- The law is codified (placed in the U.S. Code, the nation's collection of statutes).

It's not usually that simple. Many things can happen during the basic steps listed above. The next subsection covers some possibilities.

The Legislative Process Can Be Tough

People joke about how slow Congress is and how little it gets done. There's truth in the jokes, and part of it stems from how tough and time consuming the legislative process can be.

A bill's journey to become a law can be like a walk through a mine field: an explosion could go off at any step.

Committees are often where obstacles to a bill's passage start. A committee might do the following after receiving a bill:

- Seek input from agencies affected by the bill.

- Read reports about a bill's likely costs and consequences.

- Hold hearings, where people speak for or against the bill.

As well as taking time, any of those actions could affect whether some committee members support the bill.

Committees usually hold **markup** sessions, in which they debate and may change bills. When a group of people tinker with *anything*, it takes time—especially when people's agendas clash.

After markup, a bill could look very different from the original version. If a bill changes enough, it might gain some supporters but lose others.

Eventually, a committee votes on whether to send the bill to the whole chamber for consideration. If the committee votes *no*, the bill could **die in committee** (not be sent to the whole chamber)—so much for Congress's accomplishing something through that bill.

Even if a committee sends a bill to the whole chamber for consideration, the bill might not be voted on. Without a vote, a bill can't be passed.

There are different ways to prevent a vote on a bill. In the House, for example, enough members might vote to **recommit** the bill: to send it back to the committee to face who-knows-what obstacles.

In the Senate, while a bill is being debated on the floor, a senator might **filibuster**: i.e., speak for an extended time to delay or prevent a vote. The Senate's rules usually allow each senator to speak on the Senate floor *for as long as the senator wants*, mostly uninterrupted.

While one senator **holds the floor** (speaks), other senators' pet bills or other measures aren't being considered or voted on. Thus, a filibuster can "gum up the works," which is why senators often don't like other senators' filibusters. At the same time, many senators like knowing that they'll have the right to filibuster if they need to in the future.

Cloture is a way to close debate about a specific measure, like a bill or a resolution. The Senate could end a filibuster by "invoking" (voting for) cloture, but invoking cloture isn't always easy. To end debate on most types of measures requires a 3/5 vote, which is 60 senators if all 100 are present. It can be tough to get 60 senators to agree.

Filibusters don't happen in the modern House because its rules limit debate for most members.

Even if a floor vote isn't prevented, a bill in the House or Senate might endure **floor amendments** (changes made while the bill is considered on the floor of either chamber) before the vote. Amendments take time. An amendment could repel original supporters, attract new ones, and spark more debate.

Even if one chamber (the House or Senate) passes a bill and sends it to the other chamber, the second chamber might object to parts of the bill and make changes. If so, the new version would go back to the first chamber because both chambers **must pass an identical bill** for it to become law.

If the House and Senate don't agree on a bill, they could set up a **Conference Committee**—members from each chamber who meet to resolve differences. If the conference committee agrees to one version of a bill, it could go to each chamber for a floor vote.

The legislative process doesn't stop there. Even after a bill is **enrolled**—i.e., passed by both chambers—it's presented to the President, who can do one of three things:

(1) Sign it (bill becomes law).

(2) Veto it (bill doesn't become law at that point).

(3) Do nothing (bill might become law).

If the President vetoes the bill, Congress can **override the veto** by a 2/3 majority vote in each chamber. Overrides are rare because it's not easy to get that many members of Congress to agree to override a veto. The bill would probably die at that point.

If the President does nothing with a bill for 10 days after receiving it—while Congress is in session—the bill *would become law.* If the President doesn't sign the bill and Congress goes out of session (recesses) before the 10 days are up, the bill *would not* become law: that's called a **pocket veto.**

The President's role in the legislative process is in the Constitution (Article I, Section 7). You can find more details by searching online for the terms *Congress + legislative process.*

Bills **expire** if they aren't passed during the two-year Congress in which they were introduced. For example, if a member introduced a bill during the 115th Congress and the bill wasn't passed before that Congress ended, the bill would expire. In that case, the bill might be **reintroduced** during the 116th Congress— and might endure the tough process *again.*

The Framers of the Constitution didn't make it easy for Congress to pass laws. Why? Because the Framers didn't want legislators to act rashly when creating new laws. Many members of Congress may want to get things done, and quickly, but the legislative process stacks the odds against them.

Resolutions

Knowing something about resolutions can be helpful to legal researchers. A **resolution** is a form of legislative action. There are 3 types of resolutions:

(1) Joint Resolutions.

(2) Concurrent Resolutions.

(3) Simple Resolutions.

Joint resolutions are binding law and require passage by the House and Senate. Most joint resolutions are presented to the President for approval (like bills are).

Congress often uses joint resolutions for emergency or continuing appropriations. Joint resolutions are the only way that Congress can propose **amendments to the Constitution.** That type of joint resolution isn't sent to the President because presidents don't have a formal role in amending the Constitution.

Concurrent resolutions aren't binding law and aren't sent to the President, but they require passage by the House and Senate. Congress tends to use concurrent resolutions to deal with issues affecting both chambers, like scheduling Congress's adjournment and dealing with rules that apply to both chambers.

Congress also uses concurrent resolutions to express sentiments, like recognizing the anniversary of another nation's independence or condemning the actions of a terrorist group. Through a concurrent resolution, Congress might **censure a president or other official.** There aren't many limits on the sentiments that Congress can express through concurrent resolutions.

Simple resolutions are passed by only one chamber and are not binding law. Each chamber typically uses simple resolutions to deal with rules and internal affairs or to express that chamber's sentiments. The House has used simple resolutions to **impeach presidents and other officials.**

Resolutions **originating in the House** are labeled with an abbreviation + a number (the numbers below are made up):

- Joint Resolution: H.J. Res. 683.
- Concurrent Resolution: H. Con. Res. 44.
- Simple Resolution: H. Res. 1007.

Resolutions **originating in the Senate** are labeled this way:

- Joint Resolution:　　　　S.J. Res. 17.
- Concurrent Resolution:　　S. Con. Res. 53.
- Simple Resolution:　　　　S. Res. 71.

You can find more about resolutions at www.House.gov or www.Senate.gov. You can find actual resolutions that were voted on at www.Congress.gov.

House Terms & Districts

House members are elected for **2-year terms.** There are **no term limits,** so members can serve as many terms as the voters give them.

Each state gets a share of the House's 435 representatives based on the state's population. In 2019, for example, Alabama had 7 representatives, and California had 53. Most states have a big enough population to get more than one representative in the House.

A **congressional district** is a geographical area within a state, as drawn by that state's government. Districts are numbered, like Iowa's 3rd District or Georgia's 6th District. In multi-district states, the people of each district elect one House member. In smaller states that have only one district, like Alaska and Vermont, the House member represents everyone in the state.

State populations can change, so the Constitution requires a population count every 10 years. It's called the **U.S. Census.**

The Census is crucial to American democracy. Why? Because based on Census data, the federal government **reapportions** the House every 10 years—i.e., decides how many representatives each state gets based on population (Article I, Section 2). If the Census data is inaccurate, a state might get fewer (or more) representatives in the House than it should.

Some states win the reapportionment game, and some lose. After the 2010 Census, Texas gained 4 House seats, and New York lost 2 seats.

While the federal government decides how many House members a state has, the Constitution gives each state the power to draw congressional districts within its state (Article I, Section 4).

Redistricting refers to the process of redrawing districts after the Census. *Not all* states try to draw congressional districts that fairly represent all groups of people, like racial groups or members of a political party.

Gerrymandering refers to the drawing of weirdly shaped districts to benefit (or harm) one group or another, like a political group or racial group. Gerrymandering undermines the ideas of majority rule and one-person-one-vote.

That weird word relates to Massachusetts Governor Elbridge Gerry, who signed a bill in 1812 for a strange-looking redistricting plan that benefitted his political party, which harmed other parties. A newspaper political cartoon made the new district map look like a salamander. The editor added "Gerry" + part of "salamander," and came up with "Gerrymander."

Let's say that a state's major-party voters are roughly equal: about the same number of Republicans as Democrats. An example of gerrymandering would be the party that controls the state legislature drawing congressional districts so that one party's voters are crammed into fewer districts. In this example—instead of each party getting about half of the state's U.S. House seats—one party gets 80% of the seats, and the other gets only 20%.

Lawsuits have erupted over gerrymandering. The U.S. Constitution *doesn't* tell states how to draw congressional districts.

But courts have relied on constitutional provisions (e.g., 14th Amendment) when deciding some types of gerrymandering cases, like those involving disenfranchisement of racial minorities.

In 2019, the U.S. Supreme Court held that federal courts don't have jurisdiction to decide cases about **partisan gerrymandering** (gerrymandering aimed at benefitting or harming political parties).[5] The 5 so-called "conservative" justices were in the majority, and the 4 so-called "liberal" justices wanted to allow federal courts to decide such cases.

The upshot: the Supreme Court left it to Congress, the state legislatures, and the states' citizens to fight—or allow—partisan gerrymandering. The Court also gave examples of how Congress and the states might go about fighting partisan gerrymandering.

Congress hasn't yet passed laws that effectively stop partisan gerrymandering. In some states, citizens have passed constitutional amendments against partisan gerrymandering.

It's uncertain how all of that will work affect how congressional districts are redrawn after the 2020 Census, but it's possible that one of the major political parties will get a huge advantage.

Eligibility for House Membership

Finally, let's turn to House membership. To be eligible to be a House member, a person must—

- be at least 25 years old.

- be a U.S. citizen for at least 7 years.

- live in the state he or she represents.

Those requirements are in the Constitution (Article I, Section 2).

---

[5]   *Rucho v. Common Cause*, 139 S. Ct. 2484, 2508 (2019).

Senate Membership & Terms

Some people see the Senate as the rational adult, while the House plays the child. When the House passes ridiculous bills based on party agendas, the Senate has sometimes acted like the "cooler head" and stopped the nonsense by refusing to pass those bills.

The Senate *isn't always* like the Dalai Lama or Yoda. Some Senate leaders have behaved obstinately and with little apparent regard for getting the nation's business done.

The Senate has 100 members, 2 from each state. Both senators represent all people in their state, so there are **no separate Senate districts** within states, thus no gerrymandering problems.

Senators are elected to **6-year terms**. There are **no term limits**, so senators can serve as many terms as the voters give them.

About 1/3 of the senators are up for re-election every two years because the Constitution gave senators staggered terms (Article I, Section 3). That's good because six years is a long time to be stuck with the *same* 100 politicians and the *same* political party controlling the Senate.

Staggered terms allow the voters to "clean house" every two years.

To be eligible to be a senator, a person must—

- Be at least 30 years old.

- Be a U.S. citizen for at least 9 years.

- Live in the state he or she represents.

Those requirements are in the Constitution (Article I, Section 3).

Senators used to be chosen by each state's legislature. The 17th Amendment changed that. Now, *the people* of each state directly elect their senators.

All Senate members can vote on bills. Again, the U.S. Vice President—who serves as the Senate President but *isn't* elected to the Senate—can vote only to break ties. The Constitution made that so (Article I, Section 3).

Legislative Branch Agencies

Many people think of government agencies as part of the Executive Branch—like the IRS or Justice Department—and most of them are. But Congress has created agencies *within the Legislative Branch*, which support and work for Congress. Four of the better-known ones are—

- The Library of Congress.

- The Government Accountability Office.

- The Congressional Budget Office.

- The U.S. Capitol Police.

The first three listed can be useful to people doing legal or public-policy research.

The **Library of Congress** (LOC) is the largest library in the world. It hosts www.Congress.gov, where you can track legislation, check how members voted on bills, and find other information. The LOC houses the Congressional Research Service and the U.S. Copyright office. The LOC's website is www.loc.gov.

The **Government Accountability Office** (GAO) does well-researched, nonpartisan reports on all sorts of policy issues: border security, social security, healthcare, education . . . . GAO reports are at www.gao.gov.

The **Congressional Budget Office** (CBO) reports on budget and economic issues. It also estimates how much it would cost the taxpayers if a certain bill is passed. You can find tons of budget and spending information at www.cbo.gov.

The **Capitol Police** protects Congress, its staff, visitors, and various buildings and grounds. Although the Capitol Police is a law-enforcement agency, it's within the Legislative Branch (not the Executive Branch). Its website is www.uscp.gov.

Washington, D.C.: The Seat of Government

The Framers of the Constitution didn't want the nation's capital to be influenced by any state. That's why the Constitution required Congress to put the seat of government in a district that isn't in a state and to put the district under Congress's jurisdiction (Article I, Section 8). That's Washington, the District of Columbia: aka, "the District" or "D.C."

D.C. receives funds from Congress yet raises revenue through local taxes. D.C. has a mayor and a city council, but Congress can override local laws that D.C. passes.

Because D.C. isn't a state, it doesn't have senators or a full-voting member of the House. Instead (like the major U.S. territories) D.C. has a delegate to the House, whose voting rights are limited.

The 23rd Amendment gave D.C. some "electors" in the Electoral College (Chapter 3).

D.C. is a fairly big city (over 600,000 people). For some years, there has been a movement to make D.C. a state. Statehood would require amending the Constitution, which is very hard to do (Chapter 1).

The Major U.S. Territories

The five major U.S. territories and the year that each became a U.S. territory are as follows:

- American Samoa (1900).

- Guam (1898).

- Northern Mariana Islands (1947).

- Puerto Rico (1898).

- U.S. Virgin Islands (1916).

Each territory has some degree of self-governance yet is under the authority of the U.S. Government.

American Samoa is different from the other four major territories. Its citizens are U.S. nationals, *not U.S. citizens.* "Nationals" have some but not all privileges that U.S. citizens have.

The other four territories' citizens have **birthright citizenship.** If born in one of those four territories, people are U.S. citizens automatically.

Many U.S. citizens in or residents of the major territories **are U.S. taxpayers.** For example, U.S. citizens in Puerto Rico pay FICA (social security and Medicare).[6] Some must file federal income tax returns, depending on circumstances.[7] For more about taxation, search online for a territory + "tax."

Residents of American Samoa and U.S. citizens in the other four territories **can vote for their delegates** to the U.S. House.

While domiciled in a territory, U.S. citizens *can't vote* for U.S. Senators because only the states have senators (Article I, Section 3 and 17th Amendment). They also can't vote in the general election for U.S. president because only states and Washington, D.C. have

---

[6]   U.S. Internal Revenue Service, *Topic Number 903—U.S. Employment Tax in Puerto Rico,* https://www.irs.gov/taxtopics/tc903.

[7]   U.S. Internal Revenue Service, *Topic Number 901—Is a Person with Income from Puerto Rico Required to File a U.S. Federal Income Tax Return?,* https://www.irs.gov/taxtopics/tc901.

electoral college votes (more about the electoral college in Chapter 3).

U.S. citizens in some territories *can* vote in presidential **primary elections** because the major political parties in the U.S. enable them to. A territorial citizen who has U.S. citizenship could move to a state and vote in senatorial and presidential elections in that state.

The U.S. territories are addressed in Title 48 of the U.S. Code, which you can find by searching online for "Title 48" + "U.S. Code."

CHAPTER 3

Executive Branch: President & Agencies

Presidents Are Not Kings

Next time a presidential candidate promises to lower your income taxes, raise an eyebrow and think **"separation of powers."** Only Congress has the power to make laws and tax our incomes (Article I and 16th Amendment).

Presidents can sign tax-cutting bills passed by Congress. Presidents can try to persuade Congress to lower taxes. But **presidents cannot** single-handedly lower your income taxes.

Just for kicks, here are a few other examples of things that presidents can't do:

- Presidents can't declare war.

- Presidents can't borrow money on the United States' credit.

- Presidents can't decide court cases.

- Presidents can't sign treaties without Senate approval.

The bottom line: presidents can't exercise any power that the Constitution reserved for Congress or the Judicial Branch.

Presidents *can* do some things on their own but not others. That's the nature of **checks and balances**. And that's what our Founding Fathers wanted because they didn't want our government ruled by kings or other dictators.

Presidents are elected for **four years**, and there are term limits (22nd Amendment). The general limit is two terms. People who have held the Office of President for more than 2 years (like a vice president who took over for a president who had died) can be elected to only one term.

Executive Branch: Basic Functions & Size

Although presidents are not kings, the President is the head of the Executive Branch. And that position comes with a lot of power.

One function of the Executive Branch is to **execute** policies— to put them into effect. Policies are only ideas until someone executes them, which is one reason that the Executive Branch is so important.

Let's say that Congress passes a law to help certain types of small businesses by giving them loans. Congress appropriates $750 million to fund the loans.

The money wouldn't magically flow into those businesses' accounts. Someone has to set up a process for businesses to apply for the loans. Someone has to make sure that only businesses that meet Congress's criteria get the money. Someone has to deliver the money. Those kinds of practicalities are what executing policies is about.

Enforcing laws is another Executive Branch function. For example, federal law prohibits people from possessing certain drugs. Enforcing drug laws requires people to investigate and prosecute people who break the drug laws. The Executive Branch handles those things.

The Executive Branch must execute and enforce huge numbers of laws, which requires a lot of people. Not counting members of the armed services, more than 2 million people work for the Executive Branch.

Some Executive Branch agencies have offices throughout the nation. For example, the FBI has over 50 field offices that handle investigations throughout the nation. The State Department has over 25 regional offices handling passports in the U.S. and also has embassies in many foreign countries.

Presidential Powers, Limits & Duties

Powers Granted by Constitution

Among other things, Article II of the Constitution grants the President the power to—

- Command the military.
- Pardon people convicted of crimes.
- Make treaties with other nations (with Senate approval).
- Appoint many government officials.

The Constitution also limits the President's powers. For example, the President is the Commander in Chief (military), *but* only Congress can declare war. The President nominates judges for lifetime positions *but* needs the Senate's consent to confirm the nominations.

Authority Granted by Congress

The Constitution gives Congress the power to delegate authority to the Executive Branch. That makes sense because Congress relies on the Executive Branch to execute and enforce laws.

Congress can create an Executive Branch agency or change an existing agency. After the 9/11 attacks, for example, Congress created the Department of Homeland Security through statutes. Congress dictated some details and left others to the Executive Branch. For example, Congress stated the department's primary mission and laid out official positions at the top, like *Secretary* and *Deputy Secretary*.

Senate approval is required for certain presidential appointments, but Congress can give the President authority to appoint lower officers without Senate approval (Article II, Section 2).

Congress can also give an Executive Branch agency **rulemaking power**: the power to make regulations. The basic idea is that Congress sets the broader policies through statutes and gives an executive agency the authority to handle some details and logistics through regulations.

The Constitution limits which tasks Congress can delegate to agencies. For example, Congress can't give agencies the power to pass statutes because the Constitution reserves that power for Congress.

Administrative law focuses on the procedures and rules promulgated by administrative agencies. It's a complex area of law. Congress set procedures and standards regarding administrative law in the **Administrative Procedures Act** and other statutes (U.S. Code, Title 5).

Usually, agencies must publish *proposed rules*, so affected people and other members of the public are given **notice** of the proposals. Agencies often give the public a chance to **comment** and participate in the rulemaking process.

Special judges, called **Administrative Law Judges** (ALJs), often hold administrative hearings to decide disputes between an administrative agency and people affected by that agency.

ALJs have judicial-type duties but work for Executive Branch agencies. More than 30 federal agencies have ALJs. Examples include the Department of Labor, the Environmental Protection Agency, the Federal Communications Commission, and the Social Security Administration (more about ALJs in Chapter 4).

Some Duties & Limits

The Constitution gives presidents the **duty** to "take care that the laws be faithfully executed" (Article II, Section 3). Thus, a president must execute and enforce all laws, even laws that a president doesn't like.

A few presidential duties covered in Article II include—

- Being Commander in Chief of the Armed Forces.

- Informing Congress of the state of the union.

- Receiving ambassadors from other nations.

Statutes also create duties for the President, like those relating to the federal budget. For example, the Constitution says very little about the President's role in the budget, but Congress passed statutes affecting the President's role in the budget process.

Congress can impose duties and limits on presidents, as long as Congress doesn't overstep its constitutional authority. One **check** against Congress treating the President like a bill-signing puppet is the President's veto power. But there's a **counter-check**: Congress can override a veto.

Vice President: A Constitutional Hybrid

The Constitution gives the Vice President a role in the Executive *and* Legislative Branches (Articles I and II). Thus, vice presidents are hybrids.

In the Executive Branch, the Vice President's main function is to take over if the President dies, resigns, or can't fulfill the duties of office for other reasons. The Constitution doesn't give vice presidents a detailed job description.

That's why different vice presidents do the job differently. Vice presidents often handle ceremonial duties, like going to funerals or meeting with heads of other nations. Some vice presidents have publicly promoted the President's policies.

Presidents can't fire vice presidents. The Constitution gives Congress the power to remove a vice president through the impeachment process (Article I, Sections 2 and 3; Article II, Section 4).

If there is a vacancy of the Office of Vice President (e.g., if a vice president dies, resigns, or is removed from office), the President can nominate a new vice president. That nominee would take office if a majority of both houses of Congress confirmed the nomination (25th Amendment).

Congress can assign some duties to vice presidents. For example, Congress put the Vice President on the National Security Council back in the 1940s, and the Vice President is still on it today.

In the Legislative Branch, the Vice President automatically serves as the President of the Senate (Chapter 2). The Vice President doesn't vote in the Senate—except to break a tie—and doesn't usually preside over the Senate unless a vote requires a tie breaker.

Vice presidents have their own offices and staff. The Vice President's official residence is a house at the Naval Observatory in Washington, D.C.

Executive Office of the President (EOP)

As the head of the Executive Branch, a president oversees many activities and needs a large staff, which is part of the Executive Office of the President (EOP). The **White House Chief of Staff** oversees the EOP. The EOP houses various offices, including those listed below.

Examples: Offices Within the EOP

- Office of Council of Economic Advisers
- Office of National Security Advisor
- Office of Vice President
- Office of Management and Budget
- Office of the U.S. Trade Representative

The President can appoint many high-level staffers **without the Senate's approval**, like the White House Chief of Staff. Some positions require Senate approval, like the *Director of the Office of Management and Budget*.

The EOP has multiple levels of staff. One of the most visible staffers is the Press Secretary, who speaks to the public for the President.

Some staffers work in the White House building. Most work in the Eisenhower Executive Office Building (EEOB), a building near the White House.

Executive Branch Departments

Departments are the largest units of the Executive Branch. As of this writing, there are 15 departments that help execute and enforce laws. Congress can create new departments or change existing ones.

Most executive agencies fall under a department. Each department handles different policy issues. A list of departments is below, and their names give some idea of what they handle.

> ### Departments & Their Websites
>
> - **Agriculture** (usda.gov)
> - **Commerce** (commerce.gov)
> - **Defense** (defense.gov)
> - **Education** (ed.gov)
> - **Energy** (energy.gov)
> - **Health & Human Services** (hhs.gov)
> - **Homeland Security** (dhs.gov)
> - **Housing & Urban Development** (hud.gov)
> - **Interior** (doi.gov)
> - **Justice** (justice.gov)
> - **Labor** (dol.gov)
> - **State** (state.gov)
> - **Transportation** (transportation.gov)
> - **Treasury** (treasury.gov)
> - **Veterans Affairs** (va.gov)

The departments deal with broad issues. For example, the **Department of State** (a.k.a., "State Department") handles issues relating to foreign nations, including sub-issues like diplomatic efforts and passports. The **Secretary of State** heads the State Department and has layers of lower officers plus staff.

Details about what each department does and how it's organized are at each department's website.

Each department is organized differently. For example, the **Justice Department** (whose primary mission is law enforcement) has more than 50 sub-units handling sub-issues. A few examples are below:

- Bureau of Alcohol, Tobacco, & Firearms (ATF).

- Drug Enforcement Administration (DEA).

- Federal Bureau of Investigation (FBI).

- Office of Privacy & Civil Liberties.

- Tax Division.

Most department heads have the title **Secretary**, like the Secretary of Agriculture. The head of the Justice Department has the title **Attorney General**.

Presidents appoint department heads with Senate approval. The President might appoint department heads based on expertise or for other reasons, like friendship or political favors. The Senate can block unwise appointments but doesn't always do so.

Department heads serve at the President's pleasure and can be fired. Also, Congress can remove department heads from office through the impeachment process.

Presidents have some power to restructure the Executive Branch, but that power is limited by law (U.S. Code, Title 5).

The Cabinet

The President's **Cabinet** is a group of senior officials who advise the President about issues relating to those officials' positions. Because Cabinet members have the President's ear, they may influence presidential policies.

Historically, the department heads and the Vice President were the Cabinet members. But the President can reorganize the Cabinet. For example, Presidents Obama and Trump elevated some senior officials to the Cabinet whose positions had not been part of the Cabinet before.

Cabinet members can play a part in removing a president from office based on an inability to handle the duties of office (25th Amendment)—as opposed to bad conduct (impeachment: Article II, Section IV). Congress has the final say over whether a president is removed from office (more in this chapter).

Independent Agencies

"**Independent agency**" refers to an entity that (1) is in the Executive Branch but (2) *isn't* under a department and (3) *isn't* under the President's direct control. Here are a few examples:

- Federal Election Commission (FEC).

- National Labor Relations Board (NLRB).

- National Aeronautics & Space Administration (NASA).

Congress creates independent agencies by law. The purpose of making an agency independent is to reduce the influence of politics by reducing the President's control.

In many independent agencies, the decision making is done by a group, not one person. For example, Congress gave the Federal Election Commission (FEC) 6 members and required that no more than 3 members be of the same political party. The President appoints FEC commissioners with Senate approval. Commissioners serve 6-year terms, so they could outlast the President who appointed them.

FEC commissioners serve staggered terms, so two seats are open every two years. That structure is intended to prevent one president from packing the FEC with people who share the same ideology.

Independent status *doesn't guarantee* that agencies will be free from political influences. It depends on the ethics of the individuals who head an agency.

Typically, the President can fire the heads of independent agencies **for cause**, meaning if they failed to do the job or did something else wrong. It depends on what the relevant statutes say.

Presidential Directives

Overview

Three common ways for presidents to issue directives are through—

- Executive orders.
- Memoranda.
- Proclamations.

Those terms are not clearly defined or covered in the Constitution. How presidents use those devices has changed over time.

Presidents can issue directives unilaterally (alone) *but only* to exercise legitimate presidential authority granted by (1) the Constitution or (2) Congress.

There is a danger of presidents exceeding their authority when issuing executive orders, memoranda, or proclamations—for example, usurping Congress's power to legislate. Doing so would be a violation of the separation-of-powers doctrine, an issue at the heart of intense lawsuits.

Most executive orders and proclamations must be published in the Federal Register. Memoranda don't have to be published.

The next three subsections cover some details about executive orders, memoranda, and proclamations.

Executive Orders

Executive orders give instructions to Executive Branch agencies about what they should do and what their priorities should be. For example, one modern President signed an executive order instructing agencies to buy American-made goods when possible.

Executive orders are directed at the internal operations of government. But they can affect private individuals' and organizations' rights and duties by affecting *how* legislation or public policy is enforced or implemented.

Executive orders are **binding** (must be followed) if they don't violate the law. *Separation of Powers* is supposed to limit what presidents do through executive orders. For example, a president can't validly issue an executive order that appropriates more money to the Department of Education because presidents don't have the power to appropriate funds—Congress does.

Presidents have been known to cross the separation-of-powers line. If a lawsuit is filed, a court might find an executive order unlawful. Congress could invalidate some types of executive orders through legislation or could neutralize an executive order by refusing to appropriate funds necessary to implement the order.

Presidents have used executive orders in significant ways. In 1948, for example, President Truman—as Commander in Chief— signed Executive Order 9981, which called for equal treatment for people in the military "without regard to race, color, religion, or national origin."[1]

Executive orders are numbered. For example, the 44th President's last executive order was numbered EO 13764, and the 45th President's first was EO 13765.

Presidents can issue executive orders that change or revoke a past executive order, even one issued by a past president—which makes executive orders unstable. Courts have the power to determine whether executive orders are lawful (more about courts in Chapter 4).

Executive orders must be published at the Federal Register (www.federalregister.gov). Some presidents also have published executive orders at the White House website, making them easier for journalists and the public to find.

Memoranda (Plural of "Memorandum")

Like executive orders, presidential memoranda instruct executive agencies to do or not do certain things. For example, one President issued a memorandum instructing agency heads to freeze the hiring of non-military employees in the Executive Branch.

The major difference between executive orders and memoranda is that executive orders must be published in the Federal Register, while memoranda don't have to be published. Some presidents have made memoranda publicly available, anyway.

Because memoranda don't have to be published, presidents typically use them for routine actions that the public isn't interested in, like managing staff. A president might use a

---

[1]   Executive Order 9981, *Document for July 26. . .*, National Archives, https://www.archives.gov/historical-docs/todays-doc/?dod-date=726.

memorandum to issue a directive—and not publicize it—in hopes of drawing less public scrutiny.

Proclamations

Presidential **proclamations** are announcements or statements. Because there are no constitutional requirements, proclamations can address all sorts of things.

One of the most famous is the Emancipation Proclamation,[2] issued by President Abraham Lincoln, which was one step in the process of freeing slaves. The National Archives has details (www. archives.gov).

At Congress's request, President George Washington issued a proclamation to "recommend" to the people that they set aside November 26, 1789 for giving thanks for the "opportunity to establish a form of government for their safety and happiness."[3]

In modern times, proclamations are often used in a ceremonial way, like recognizing a person or issue. For example, a presidential proclamation proclaimed one day to be *Military Spouse Day*.

Some presidents use proclamations to issue pardons for people convicted of crimes. Presidents have also used proclamations to address trade or foreign affairs issues.

While executive orders have the force of law, proclamations don't unless authorized by Congress. Proclamations are published in the Federal Register. Some presidents also publish proclamations at the White House website.

---

[2]   Some people refer to the Emancipation Proclamation as an executive order, though it was denominated as a *proclamation*, which the State Department later numbered "95." National Archives, *The Emancipation Proclamation*, https://www. archives.gov/exhibits/featured-documents/emancipation-proclamation.

[3]   National Archives, *Thanksgiving Proclamation, 3 October 1789*, https:// founders.archives.gov/documents/Washington/05-04-02-0091.

Electing the President & Vice President

Political Parties & Ballot Access

Political parties play a huge role in electing presidents. The two major parties are the Democrats and the Republicans. **Third-party candidates** are members of other parties. **Independent candidates** aren't part of a formal party—confusing because there is a party called the "American Independent Party."

Each major party has a **national-level organization**: the Republican National Committee (RNC) and the Democratic National Committee (DNC). The major parties also have **state-level organizations**, like the North Dakota Republican Party and the Wyoming Democrats. The same is true of some smaller parties, like the Libertarian and Green parties.

Ballot access refers to candidates' ability to get on a state's general-election ballot so people can easily vote for them. State and federal laws affect candidates' ballot access.

In the 2016 presidential election, the candidates of only 3 parties made it onto all 50 states' ballots: Democratic, Republican, and Libertarian. The Green Party candidate was on the ballot in only 44 states and Washington, D.C.

Third-party candidates tend to get fewer votes. Here's the Election 2016 vote count (from www.fec.gov):

- Democrat (Clinton):   65,853,516
- Republican (Trump):   62,984,825
- Libertarian (Johnson):   4,489,221
- Green (Stein):   1,457,216

Third-party candidates can have a significant impact on elections, even if they don't win. First, they get media attention and can influence public opinion. Second, they might draw votes away from major-party candidates.

For example, some people who voted for Gary Johnson in the 2016 election *might* have instead voted for Donald Trump if Johnson had not run. The same could be said about Jill Stein and Hillary Clinton. We can't know how many votes a third-party candidate took away from a major candidate because we don't know how many voters would have refused to vote for a major-party candidate if the third-party candidate hadn't run.

Basic Overview of Electoral Process

The People directly elect members of Congress. It *seems* like we directly elect presidents and vice presidents because the candidates' names are on the ballots, **but we don't.**

By voting for a "ticket" (the presidential and vice-presidential candidates who run for office as a team), we're actually voting for a **group of electors** (people) in our state whom we want to vote for our candidates through the **Electoral College**, which meets more than a month after Election Day.

It sounds weird because it is (more about the Electoral College in the next subsection). Here are the **basic steps in the electoral process:**

- Political parties hold primaries or caucuses in states and some U.S. territories.
- Political parties hold national nominating conventions.
- States hold the General Election (November).
- Electoral College votes to elect the president (and vice president).
- Congress counts the Electoral College votes.

General Election

Election Day and Before

Election Day for presidential candidates and their running mates (vice-presidential candidates) happens every 4 years on the Tuesday after the first Monday in November. That date is set by statute (3 U.S. Code § 1).

Election Day happens after the major political parties (and some smaller parties) choose their presidential candidates. Each political party has its own rules for choosing its candidate for president. The major parties hold national conventions after state- and territory-level primaries or caucuses.

Primaries are pretty straightforward. They are public elections, conducted by local governments within a state. Most states have primaries.

Caucuses are private gatherings conducted by political parties at the state level. Many people complain about caucuses because the candidate for president is chosen by a relatively small group of party-insiders, instead of the voting public.

Both primaries and caucuses give state-level parties some say over which candidate the national-level party will choose to run in the general election.

A party's **national convention** is where the national-level political party decides which candidate will be the presidential nominee for that party: i.e., which candidate will run in the general election. Each party's delegates from the states go to the party's national convention.

Usually, the nominee is the one who wins a majority of the votes in the state primaries and caucuses, but not necessarily. It depends on a political party's rules about choosing a candidate.

Electoral College

The **Electoral College** isn't a place. It's a process involving a group of people who vote to elect a president and vice president.

The Electoral College has 538 **electors**, people from the states and Washington, D.C. Each state political party chooses its own "slate" (group) of electors. The electors are supposed to vote for that party's presidential and vice-presidential candidates if those candidates win the state's general election. Party rules and state law affect the process for choosing a state's electors for the Electoral College.

Why 538 electors? Each state gets the same number of electors as the number of members the state has in Congress. In 2016, for example, Virginia had 11 House members and 2 senators: thus, 13 electors in the Electoral College.

There are **535** *state* electors: the same number as all voting members of Congress. The 23rd Amendment (1961) gave Washington D.C. some Electoral College votes. In 2016, D.C. had **3** electoral votes: thus, **535 + 3 = 538**.

On Election Day, the voters in each state vote for a presidential candidate's **"ticket,"** which includes that candidate's **running mate** (person running for vice president). The presidential and vice-presidential candidates are a package deal.

Most states[4] and Washington, D.C. have a **winner-takes-all** system for allocating electoral votes to candidates. For example, let's say that there are only two candidates. If one candidate wins 52% of a state's popular vote and the other candidate wins 48%, the candidate who won 52% would take *all* of that state's electoral votes, and the other candidate would get zero.

---

[4]   As of July 2019, Maine and Nebraska did not have a winner-take-all system.

In the December directly after Election Day, the Electoral College "meets." The 538 electors don't gather in one place for cocktails and finger food.

Instead, electors go to their state capitol to cast their votes for president (and vice president). The candidate who gets at least **270 electoral votes** (more than half of 538) wins the Presidency.

Why such a complex system for electing presidents? Because the Founding Fathers disagreed about how to elect a president. Some wanted *the people* to directly elect presidents, some wanted Congress to do it, and some wanted the states to do it. The Electoral College was a compromise (Article II, Section 1 and 12th Amendment).

Popular Vote Versus Electoral Votes

The **popular vote** is the number of votes cast by *the people*. More than 130 million people voted in the 2016 presidential election, for example.

Electoral votes are those cast by the 538 members of the Electoral College. *Usually*, the candidate who wins the popular vote also wins the electoral votes. So far, 5 presidents have taken office **without winning the popular vote:**[5]

- John Quincy Adams (1824).

- Rutherford Hayes (1876).

- Benjamin Harrison (1888).

---

[5] John Q. Adams won through a contingent election of the U.S. House of Representatives (12th Amendment) because no candidate had won a majority of electoral votes: his opponent had won more electoral and popular votes. Hayes was put into an office through a commission appointed by Congress (the Compromise of 1877). Harrison, Bush, and Trump lost the popular vote but won a majority of the electoral votes.

- George W. Bush (2000).

- Donald Trump (2016).

The 2020 Census is likely to change the number of House members that some states have: i.e., so some states may gain seats and some may lose seats. If the number of House seats changes in a state, so does the state's number of electoral votes. For example, after the 2010 Census, Florida gained 2 electoral votes, and Illinois lost 1 electoral vote.[6]

Changing the Presidential Election Process

Majority rule and **one-person-one-vote** are American ideals— basic principles of democracy. Many Americans view the Electoral College as anti-democracy because a candidate can lose the popular vote and still become president.

That's why some people want to change the winner-take-all approach that most states take when awarding electoral votes. Abolishing the Electoral College would require amending the Constitution, which is hard to do (this book, chapter 1).

People averse to the Electoral College have proposed changing *states'* systems. That's possible because each state can choose how to award its electoral votes. But **not all proposed "reforms" would promote majority rule** or one-person-one-vote.

For example, under the "Congressional District System,"[7] (1) one electoral vote goes to the presidential candidate who wins the popular vote in *each congressional district* and (2) the remaining two electoral votes go to the candidate who gets the most votes *statewide.*[8]

---

[6]   U.S. Census Bureau, *2010 Apportionment Results*, https://www.census.gov/population/apportionment/data/2010_apportionment_results.html.

[7]   Maine and Nebraska use a Congressional District System.

[8]   National Conference of State Legislatures, *The Electoral College*, http://www.ncsl.org/research/elections-and-campaigns/the-electoral-college.aspx.

Unfortunately, some states' congressional districts are **gerrymandered** (this book, chapter 2), giving one political party a disproportionately big advantage over another. Thus, the Congressional District System could easily undermine the democratic ideals of majority rule and one-person-one-vote.

The proposed "Whole Number Proportional System" would give candidates electoral votes based on the proportion of a state's popular vote that each candidate wins. But **there's a problem**: numbers are rounded up (or down) because electoral votes have to be in whole numbers, per the Constitution.

For example, one state has **4 electoral votes** and follows the "Whole Number Proportional System." Let's do some simple math:

- Candidate A gets **60%** of the state's popular vote—

    (a) $60\% \times 4 = 2.4$

    (b) 2.4 *rounds down* to **2 electoral votes**.

- Candidate B gets **40%** of the state's popular vote—

    (a) $40\% \times 4 = 1.6$

    (b) 1.6 *rounds up* to **2 electoral votes**.

Each candidate would get 2 electoral votes, though one had a majority of the popular vote and the other had a minority.

In short, the results would be **disproportionate**—the awarding of electoral votes would not reflect the popular vote or the majority's will. That's a big flaw in the system if the goals are majority rule and one-person-one-vote.

Another proposal is the "National Popular Vote" bill. Basically, all states that pass the bill agree to award all of their electoral votes to the presidential candidate who wins the nationwide popular vote.

For the bill to become effective, enough states would have to pass the bill so that those states collectively have at least 270 electoral votes. Reportedly, 15 states and Washington, D.C. have passed the bill—which collectively have 196 electoral votes.

To learn more about the pros and cons of that proposed system, search online for "National Popular Vote bill," and please read differing opinions.

Removing Presidents (or Others) from Office

Impeachment Process: Wrongdoing

Impeachment is about crimes or other wrongdoing. The Constitution says that presidents and other "civil officers" can be removed from office if impeached and convicted of "Treason, Bribery, or other high Crimes and Misdemeanors" (Article II, Section 4). The Constitution *doesn't say* what qualifies as "high crimes and misdemeanors."

In this context, **impeach** means to bring charges that accuse someone of wrongdoing. Impeachment is only one step in the process of removing a president from office.

Articles of Impeachment contain the written charge(s) against a president. The Constitution gives the House the power to impeach (Article I, Section 2). The House can impeach a president by adopting Articles of Impeachment through a majority vote of the House members who are present.

If a president is impeached, the Senate holds an **impeachment trial**. It takes a 2/3 vote of the Senate members present to **convict** a president (find him or her guilty). If convicted, a president is removed from office.

Only three presidents have been impeached. The House impeached Andrew Johnson in 1868 partly because he had removed an official from office without Congress's approval. The Senate **acquitted** (didn't convict) Johnson, so he stayed in office.

The House impeached Bill Clinton in 1998. The charges related to his false testimony about a sexual affair he'd had with a woman. The Senate acquitted Clinton.

The House impeached Donald Trump in 2019. The two articles of impeachment charged him with (1) abuse of power and (2) obstruction of Congress. The Senate **acquitted** (didn't convict) Trump, so he stayed in office

Richard Nixon was on the road to impeachment over the Watergate cover-up. The proceedings began in 1974, but Nixon resigned before the process was complete—before the House even held an impeachment vote.

The 25th Amendment: Removing Presidents

Death, Resignation, or Removal

The 25th Amendment covers what happens if a president dies in office, resigns, or is removed (by impeachment or another way). On a president's death, resignation, or removal, the Vice President becomes President (25th Amendment, Section 1).

Presidents Removing Themselves

Presidents can resign from office, like Richard Nixon did. Resignation is permanent.

The 25th Amendment gives presidents a way to **temporarily remove themselves** from office if they're "unable to discharge the powers and duties" of office (25th Amendment, Section 3). For example, President George W. Bush temporarily transferred his power to his Vice President before going under anesthesia for a medical procedure.

To remove himself or herself, the President must send to the House Speaker and the Senate President Pro Tempore **a letter** declaring that the President is unable to discharge the powers and duties of office. Then the Vice President takes over as Acting President.

To reclaim the powers, the President must send to the House Speaker and the Senate President Pro Tempore a letter stating that the President is again able to handle the powers and duties.

Other People Removing Presidents

The 25th Amendment gives a **special group** of officials (the Vice President plus "a majority of either the principal officers of the executive departments or of such other body as Congress may by law provide") a way to remove a president who isn't able "to discharge the powers and duties of office" (25th Amendment, Section 4). To do that, the special group must send to the House Speaker and Senate President Pro Tempore a letter stating that the President is unable to handle the duties of office. Then the Vice President takes over as Acting President.

After the special group sends a removal letter to the House Speaker and Senate President Pro Tempore, the President could take over again by sending to the House Speaker and Senate President Pro Tempore a letter stating that the President is able again. If nobody prevents it, the President would go back to work.

But it could go differently. The special group could send to the House Speaker and Senate President Pro Tempore *another letter*, stating that the President really isn't able to handle the powers and duties of office.

If that happens, Congress has a limited time to decide—by a 2/3 vote of each chamber—that the President is "unable to discharge the powers and duties of his office."

In that case, the President would be removed from office, and the Vice President would continue as Acting President. If Congress doesn't vote within the allotted time to remove the President, the President would "resume the powers and duties of his office."

Order of Succession: Who Takes Over

The Vice President is the first in line to take over if the President dies, resigns, or is removed from office. But what if the Vice President isn't able to serve when that happens?

That's what the **order of succession** is about, also called "line of succession." It covers which officials would step in and in what order. The order of succession is—

1. Vice President (per Article II, Section 1 and 25th Amendment).

2. Speaker of the House.

3. Senate President Pro Tempore.

4. Secretary of State.

5. Secretary of the Treasury.

6. Secretary of Defense.

7. Attorney General.

8. Secretary of the Interior.

9. Secretary of Agriculture.

10. Secretary of Commerce.

11. Secretary of Labor.

12. Secretary of Health and Human Services.

13. Secretary of Housing and Urban Development.

14. Secretary of Transportation.

15. Secretary of Energy.

16. Secretary of Education.

17. Secretary of Veterans Affairs.

18. Secretary of Homeland Security.

Let's say that a president and vice president died or became incapacitated at the same time. In that case, the Speaker of the House would step in.

What if the Speaker couldn't take over for some reason? In that case, the Senate's President Pro Tempore would step in. If that person couldn't take over, then the Secretary of State would be next in line. And so on.

Because the order of succession is set by statute,[9] the order can change if Congress wants to change it.

Requirements for Being a President

Of course, a person is required to win some elections to become president. In addition, to be eligible to be a president, a person must be—

- At least 35 years old.

- A natural-born citizen of the U.S. (born in the U.S.).

- A U.S. resident for at least 14 years.

List of U.S. Presidents

The table on the next page lists all U.S. presidents from #1–#45.

---

[9]   3 U.S. Code § 19.

U.S. Presidents

1. George Washington (1789-97)	24. Grover Cleveland (1893-97)
2. John Adams (1797-1801)	25. William McKinley (1897-1901)
3. Thomas Jefferson (1801-09)	26. Theodore Roosevelt (1901-09)
4. James Madison (1809-17)	27. William H. Taft (1909-13)
5. James Monroe (1817-25)	28. Woodrow Wilson (1913-21)
6. John Quincy Adams (1825-29)	29. Warren Harding (1921-23)
7. Andrew Jackson (1829-37)	30. Calvin Coolidge (1923-29)
8. Martin Van Buren (1837-41)	31. Herbert Hoover (1929-33)
9. William H. Harrison (1841)	32. Franklin Roosevelt (1933-45)
10. John Tyler (1841-45)	33. Harry Truman (1945-53)
11. James K. Polk (1845-49)	34. Dwight Eisenhower (1953-61)
12. Zachary Taylor (1849-50)	35. John F. Kennedy (1961-63)
13. Millard Fillmore (1850-53)	36. Lyndon Johnson (1963-69)
14. Franklin Pierce (1853-57)	37. Richard Nixon (1969-74)
15. James Buchanan (1857-61)	38. Gerald Ford (1974-77)
16. Abraham Lincoln (1861-65)	39. Jimmy Carter (1977-81)
17. Andrew Johnson (1865-69)	40. Ronald Reagan (1981-89)
18. Ulysses Grant (1869-77)	41. George H.W. Bush (1989-93)
19. Rutherford Hayes (1877-81)	42. Bill Clinton (1993-2001)
20. James Garfield (1881)	43. George W. Bush (2001-09)
21. Chester Arthur (1881-85)	44. Barack Obama (2009-17)
22. Grover Cleveland (1885-89)	45. Donald Trump (2017-)
23. Benjamin Harrison (1889-93)	

CHAPTER 4

Judicial Branch: Courts & Agencies

Roles & Functions

Checks & Balances

As part of the system of checks and balances, the Judicial Branch has the power of **judicial review**, meaning that courts "say what the law is."[1] Judicial review enables courts to—

- Interpret the Constitution and other laws.

- Decide whether laws are unconstitutional.

- Decide whether government action is illegal.

Courts don't have the power to make public policy (Congress does that by passing laws). **But** how a court interprets any law can affect public policy—it's unavoidable.

For example, the Constitution's 1st Amendment protects your freedom of speech against government censoring but *doesn't* say

---

[1] *Marbury v. Madison*, 5 U.S. 137, 177 (1803).

what "speech" means. Does it include words you published online? Words on a T-shirt? Artwork?

How courts have interpreted the word "speech" in the 1st Amendment determines which types of expressions a government can regulate. For example, some artworks involving sexuality (like films or paintings) get 1st Amendment protection, but child pornography doesn't.

As long as Congress passes any unclear laws, courts will have to interpret some of them. It's part of our courts' duties. And people will continue debating and getting upset over how courts interpret laws.

As well as reviewing laws, courts can review government actions. For example, a court might find that an FBI's raid on a suspect's home was illegal. A court might find that the Veterans Administration's cutting off someone's benefits violated a statute, a regulation, or the Constitution.

Those are a few ways the Judicial Branch acts as a check on the other branches, but checks and balances work in multiple directions. For example, Congress checks the Judicial Branch through the power to remove judges from the courts.

Enforcing the Law & Resolving Disputes

The Executive Branch enforces the law, and the Judicial Branch plays a role. That's true in criminal and civil cases.

A **criminal case** aims at punishing someone who is accused of committing a crime. Crimes are considered offenses against the government and society, like murder and robbery. Only certain government entities—*not* individuals—can prosecute criminal cases. Punishment for committing a crime could include loss of freedom (e.g., jail time), a fine (money), or both.

Let's say that Darla the Drug Dealer sells illegal drugs online to people in several states. The Executive Branch investigates and prosecutes Darla. If the case goes to trial, it would happen in court (Judicial Branch). The court might convict Darla and impose a sentence, like jail time. The Executive Branch would make sure that Darla served the sentence.

Civil cases involve laws or legal duties that need to be enforced, but they don't involve loss of freedom as a possible punishment. For example, if a driver has a legal duty to drive a car carefully, the law might require someone who negligently causes an accident to provide a **remedy**, like paying the injured party's medical bills. Unless the negligent driver also committed a crime while causing the accident, there won't be jail time or other criminal penalties.

The **parties** in a court case are the people (or entities) that sue or are sued. Almost anyone can be a party in a civil case, and almost anyone can bring a civil suit (or case or action). For example, you might sue a blogger for publishing things about you that were nasty and false. A business might sue another business for failing to keep a promise in a contract.

Courts are like referees, but they don't step in whenever they see injustice. To get a court involved in a situation, someone has to bring a case to court.

In a civil case, the court would resolve the dispute by deciding—based on the law—who was right, who was wrong, and what should happen. For example, a court might order the nasty blogger to compensate you by paying you money.

There are rules for criminal and civil trials, like rules controlling which evidence is allowed at trial. Part of a court's job is to make sure that the rules and proper procedures are followed during the litigation process.

Sources of Judicial Branch's Power

The Constitution established only one court: the U.S. Supreme Court (Article III, Section 1). The Constitution also defines some of the Supreme Court's **jurisdiction**—legal ability to hear cases.

If a court doesn't have jurisdiction over a case, the court doesn't have legal authority to pass judgment on that case. Congress has the power to affect some aspects of the Supreme Court's jurisdiction (Article III, Section 2).

Congress also has the power to establish "inferior courts" (Articles I and III). Congress created the earliest form of our court system through the Judiciary Act of 1789. Other statutes have changed the system over the past 200+ years. The next few sections cover basics about court systems and specific federal courts.

Basics About Court Systems

Federal Court System

Full judicial power includes the ability to decide cases in which someone's life, liberty, or property is at stake. Not all federal courts have full judicial power.

The main U.S. (federal) courts that have full judicial power are—

- The U.S. Supreme Court.
- U.S. Circuit Courts of Appeal.
- U.S. District Courts.

The **district courts** (trial courts) hold trials. During a trial, either a judge or a jury decides whether someone is guilty in a criminal case or liable (at fault) in a civil case.

The **circuit courts of appeal** (appellate courts) are higher up the chain. They hear appeals on cases from lower courts and tribunals.

As the highest court, the **Supreme Court** has the last word about a particular case or law. Lower courts must follow Supreme Court decisions. The Supreme Court can review cases from the circuit courts of appeal but also serves other functions.

Types of federal courts are covered in more detail in this chapter. Also, the federal court system's main website has information about courts, cases, and history (www.uscourts.gov).

State Courts & Their Relationship to Federal Courts

As well as their own laws, the states have their own court systems, but the courts are named and organized differently. In New York and Maryland, for example, the highest court is the "Court of Appeals." In most states, the highest court is called "Supreme Court," like the Utah Supreme Court.

Florida has two levels of trial courts: circuit courts and county courts. Texas has more levels of trial courts, including district courts, county courts, probate courts, and municipal courts

State court systems are separate from the federal court system, but the systems do intersect. A state's highest court has the final word about interpretation of *state* law.

The U.S. Supreme Court can overrule a state court's interpretation of *federal law* (including the U.S. Constitution).

For information on a particular state's court system, search online for the state + "court system."

Federal Judges: Independence & Terms

The Framers of the Constitution wanted to create an **independent judiciary**—they didn't want courts to be vulnerable to politicians' or other people's influence. Independence promotes fairness, justice, and the Rule of Law.

At least two constitutional requirements were intended to promote federal judges' independence:

- Life appointments.

- Salary protection.

The main types of federal judges are appointed for life during good behavior. Basically, they can stay on the court until they resign, die, or are removed.

Because of life appointments, judges can outlast elected politicians. If federal judges were elected instead of appointed, they might feel pressured to decide cases based on politicians' or voters' agendas.

Because a judge's salary can't be reduced after the judge takes office, politicians can't use personal income to pressure judges to decide cases in certain ways.

The President appoints many federal judges, in some cases with Senate approval. The Constitution and some statutes cover the appointment process for different types of judges.

Federal judges can be removed from office through impeachment. If the House impeaches and the Senate convicts a judge, the judge would be removed from "the bench" (i.e., the court).

Over the past 200+ years, 15 federal judges were impeached, and only 8 were convicted (removed). Below are a few examples of conduct that resulted in judges being removed:

- Being drunk in court.

- Tax evasion.

- Perjury (lying under oath).

- Receiving a bribe.

Courts' Effect on Law & Public Policy

Legal Decisions & Political Consequences

Congress and the President make political decisions. But courts' rulings in some types of cases have political consequences— it's unavoidable.

Public policy involves choices about whose interests are protected. Often, the following parties' interests clash:

- Government vs. people.

- Government vs. businesses.

- People vs. businesses.

- Wealthy people vs. poor people.

The outcomes of some court cases affect whether the law protects one of those parties' interests more than another's.

A judge's political ideology should *not* influence a court's decisions. In reality, some judges' rulings consistently favor certain interests over others. For example, some judges consistently rule to protect ordinary people's rights against government power. Other judges tend to favor governments or big businesses.

Labels: Conservative, Liberal, Moderate, Activist

Some people label judges and courts based on how they tend to rule. The labels **aren't fully reliable**, but many media and politicians use the labels anyway.

So-called **conservative** judges are those who tend to protect government's power or big businesses' interests over ordinary people's interests. So-called **liberal** judges tend to favor ordinary people's interests over government's power or big businesses' interests.

Moderate is a harder label to pin down. It seems to mean hard to predict.

Activist is another iffy label. It refers to judges seen as *actively* trying to affect public policy through court cases. Judges of all ideologies have, at times, behaved like "activists." Usually, people hurl the word "activist" at a judge if they don't like the effect of that judge's ruling.

It's good to understand what people mean when using those loose terms. But those terms don't have definite meanings.

Precedents & Stare Decisis

A **precedent** is a rule or principle stated in a past court case. Consider two voting-rights cases as examples. In *Breedlove v. Suttles* (1937), the U.S. Supreme Court interpreted the Constitution as allowing states to require people to pay a **poll tax** (money) in order to vote in elections for state and local officials.

Poll taxes made it hard for many people to vote. At the time of the *Breedlove* case, America was still in the Great Depression. Many people had to choose between spending money to vote or to buy food.

The 24th Amendment (1964) abolished poll taxes for federal elections, but the *Breedlove* precedent allowed states to charge poll taxes for *state* elections. In *Harper v. Virginia State Board of Elections* (1966), the Supreme Court reversed the *Breedlove* case and set a new precedent—poll taxes are unconstitutional for all elections.

Stare Decisis is a principle that compels courts to follow their own precedents: to rule the same way today as they did in similar past cases. Sometimes, courts reverse their own precedents, as the Supreme Court did in the *Breedlove* case.

Lower courts must follow the precedents of higher courts within the jurisdiction. Precedents can change, but lower courts can't change a higher court's precedents.

Stare Decisis promotes fairness and predictability by increasing the chances that the law will be enforced similarly for all people. By following precedents, courts protect the Rule of Law.

District Courts (Trial Courts)

What District Courts Do

Among other things, district courts hold trials to resolve disputes among parties. Whether criminal or civil cases, trial courts determine—

- What happened (the "facts" or "truth").

- Whether a party violated a law or legal duty.

- What the law requires the parties to do.

At trial, both parties usually argue that the facts (truth), the law, or both are on their side. The parties typically present **evidence** to prove their case, like witness testimony.

Sometimes, lawyers challenge a law's validity at trial. District courts have the power to decide whether a law is constitutional.

District courts also have the power to issue orders. A **court order** directs someone to do something or not do something. Here are a few examples of what courts do through orders:

- Set trial dates.

- Impose sentences (criminal cases).

- Restrain a person from going near someone.

- Require a person to do something.

Courts have the power to hold people in **contempt of court** for not following court orders. For example, a court might impose a fine or send someone to jail for disobeying a court order.

Trials & Your Rights

Jury Trials

In a jury trial, jurors decide **questions of fact**—meaning which party's version of the "facts" is true. Did a defendant actually rob a bank? Did a defendant manufacture a dangerous product?

Judges decide **questions of law**, meaning how the law should be interpreted or applied. Was the search of a criminal defendant's house legal? Is a law unconstitutional? Judges also instruct the jury about the law that applies in a case. Here's what typically happens at a jury trial:

- The parties argue their cases, usually through lawyers.

- The judge instructs the jury.

- The jury deliberates (considers evidence).

- The jury renders a verdict (states the decision).

In a criminal case, the judge usually decides the sentence based on sentencing laws. In a civil case where a party seeks **damages** (money paid for harm suffered), the jury usually decides the amount of damages.

Judges can **set aside** (invalidate) a jury's verdict in some circumstances, but it doesn't happen often. In criminal cases, judges can set aside a guilty verdict but *not* a not-guilty verdict.

Bench Trials

In a **bench trial**, there is no jury. The judge decides questions of both fact and law. The judge decides the outcome of the case.

Some parties prefer a judge over a jury. In complex civil cases, for example, the parties might think a judge will better understand the evidence. In a criminal case, a defendant might prefer a judge because, for example, the defendant feels that a jury would be biased due to pre-trial media coverage.

Constitutional Rights Regarding Trials

The Constitution's 5th, 6th, and 8th Amendments address some of our rights regarding criminal cases. The 7th Amendment covers civil trials.

Among other things, the **5th Amendment** protects you against—

- Being punished twice for the same crime.

- Being forced to testify against yourself (criminal).

- Being deprived of life, liberty or property. without due process of law.

The Constitution doesn't say what "due process of law" means. Congress, the Executive Branch, and the courts have played roles in defining which legal processes must be followed before a government deprives a person of rights, freedoms, or property.

The **6th Amendment** gives criminal defendants the right to a jury trial in criminal cases. Courts have interpreted that right as *not* applying to petty crimes, like some traffic laws. The 6th Amendment also gives criminal defendants the right—

- To be informed of the nature of the charges.

- To confront witnesses against the defendant.

- To compel witnesses to testify (subpoena).

- To have assistance of counsel (a lawyer).

- To a speedy, public trial.

The Constitution doesn't say what "speedy" means. It also says nothing about the *quality* of "assistance of counsel." Must the lawyer have certain skills? What about a lawyer who slams vodka shots before trial?

If you're curious about how some courts have ruled on the right to counsel, search online for "ineffective assistance of counsel cases." What you find might surprise you.

The **8th Amendment** prohibits—

- Excessive fines.

- Cruel and unusual punishment.

- Excessive bail.

The Constitution doesn't say what "excessive" and "cruel and unusual" mean, so courts have had to interpret those terms (i.e., decide what the terms mean).

The **7th Amendment** gives people the right to a jury trial in certain types of civil cases. Parties can waive their jury-trial rights and choose a bench trial.

Types & Appointment of Judges in District Courts

The Constitution gives **full district court judges** life appointments during good behavior. Presidents appoint district judges with Senate approval.

Federal **magistrate judges** work in district courts and help with the workload. Magistrates perform tasks delegated by the courts, as allowed by law.

Bankruptcy courts are special units within district courts. **Bankruptcy judges** work for district courts and hear bankruptcy cases. Congress decides how many bankruptcy judges are in each district.

Magistrate and bankruptcy judges don't have life appointments or salary protection. They are appointed for limited terms by courts (not the President).

Number, Location & Jurisdiction

There are 94 federal district courts (2019). Every state and certain U.S. territories, like Puerto Rico, have at least one.

Congress divided some states into geographical districts. For example, Georgia has 3 federal judicial districts: Northern, Middle, and Southern District of Georgia. Some smaller states and territories constitute one district, like the District of Delaware and the District of the Virgin Islands.

The Constitution gives Congress the power to set district courts' jurisdiction.[2] Below are three examples of the types of cases district courts have jurisdiction over:

- Cases involving the U.S. Constitution or statutes.
- Cases involving patents or copyrights.
- Certain types of cases involving citizens of different states.

Geography plays a part in jurisdiction. If someone commits a federal crime in Gainesville, Florida, the case would likely be tried

---

[2] The U.S. Code covers district courts' jurisdiction (Title 28, Part IV).

in the U.S. District Court for the Northern District of Florida because Gainesville is within the Northern District.

Circuit Courts of Appeals (Appellate Courts)

What Circuit Courts of Appeals Do and Don't Do

The federal circuit courts of appeals are **appellate courts**: they hear appeals, as opposed to conducting trials. Most federal circuit courts review decisions of lower courts and other tribunals, as well as decisions of federal administrative agencies. Typically, appellate courts—

- Don't re-try cases.

- Don't review new evidence.

- Don't have witnesses or juries.

Appellate courts usually decide whether legal errors occurred at the lower court or tribunal, like whether the law was applied incorrectly or the proceedings were conducted in error. In some cases, a party has argued on appeal that a law applied by the lower court was unconstitutional.

If a lower court made an error, an appellate court could **remand** the case (send it back to the lower court for the error to be corrected). In some situations, appellate courts have ordered new trials.

Appellate courts don't go around looking for cases. To have a case heard on appeal, a party must petition an appellate court.

Trials Versus Appeals

At **trial**, the lawyers on each side take turns arguing their case in court. They typically question their witnesses, cross-examine the other side's witnesses, and present other evidence.

If a case is appealed, the appellate court receives a **record** of the proceedings in the trial court. The appellate court usually is limited to reviewing what is in the record.

In an **appeal**, the parties on each side of a case submit a **brief** to the court—a written document stating the party's arguments and the legal basis for the case. Sometimes, appellate courts decide a case based only on the briefs, without lawyers appearing in court.

Sometimes, appellate courts allow the parties to make **oral arguments** in court. During oral arguments, there is no testimony from witnesses. Lawyers from each side take turns standing before the judges and arguing the case. Judges often interrupt lawyers to fire questions at them.

At some point after oral arguments, the judges deliberate on the case. Eventually, and it can take months, the appellate court will rule on the case and produce a written opinion. (Side note: appellate court opinions are heavily featured in the case books that law students study.)

Circuit Courts' Effect on Law & Public Policy

A circuit court's ruling on a legal issue is the final word within the circuit, unless the Supreme Court invalidates the ruling. Because the Supreme Court hears very few cases, most circuit courts' rulings stand.

Thus, circuit courts often have an impact on public policy within their circuits.

Where the Circuits Are

So far, Congress has created 13 federal appellate circuits: 12 encompass some states and territories, and one hears certain types of cases regardless of geography. Below is a list of the federal appellate circuits:

- **1st Circuit**: Maine, Massachusetts, New Hampshire, Puerto Rico, Rhode Island.

- **2nd Circuit**: Connecticut, New York, Vermont.

- **3rd Circuit**: Delaware, New Jersey, Pennsylvania, U.S. Virgin Islands.

- **4th Circuit**: Maryland, North Carolina, South Carolina, Virginia, West Virginia.

- **5th Circuit**: Louisiana, Mississippi, Texas.

- **6th Circuit**: Kentucky, Michigan, Ohio, Tennessee.

- **7th Circuit**: Illinois, Indiana, Wisconsin.

- **8th Circuit**: Arkansas, Iowa, Minnesota, Missouri, Nebraska, North Dakota, South Dakota.

- **9th Circuit**: Alaska, Arizona, California, Guam, Hawaii, Idaho, Montana, Nevada, Northern Mariana Islands, Oregon, Washington.

- **10th Circuit**: Colorado, Kansas, New Mexico, Oklahoma, Utah, Wyoming.

- **11th Circuit**: Alabama, Florida, Georgia.

- **D.C. Circuit**: Washington, D.C.

- **Federal Circuit**: entire U.S., certain types of cases.

You can find out more about any circuit court by searching online for the specific court: for example, "U.S. federal court 9th circuit."

The U.S. Supreme Court

Supreme Court Justices

Judges on the Supreme Court are called "Justices." Currently, there are positions for 9 Justices on that Court: the Chief Justice and 8 Associate Justices. Congress decides the number of Justices by statute.[3]

---

[3]   28 U.S. Code § 1.

The Constitution gives presidents the power to appoint Justices, with Senate approval, but *doesn't* list qualifications for Justices. Yes, a President could nominate someone who has no legal training, but the Senate might not confirm that appointment. Checks and balances.

Presidents tend to appoint people to the U.S. Supreme Court who have served as judges or have a solid legal background. The current Justices' bios are at www.supremecourt.gov.

What the Supreme Court Does

Mostly, the Supreme Court acts as an appellate court, like the circuit courts but at a higher level. The Supreme Court reviews cases from circuit courts and other federal courts. It can review state court cases involving federal law.

Below are examples of the types of cases the Supreme Court has jurisdiction over:

- Cases arising under the Constitution, other federal laws, or U.S. treaties.
- Controversies in which the U.S. Government is a party.
- Controversies between two or more U.S. states.

The Constitution gives Congress the power to affect some aspects of the Supreme Court's jurisdiction (Article III, Section 2).

Supreme Court's Effect on Public Policy

The Supreme Court affects law and public policy no matter what that Court does. When the Court chooses to *not* hear a case, the Court is allowing a lower court's decision to stand—which affects law and policy.

When the Supreme Court interprets the U.S. Constitution in a case, that ruling stands unless the Supreme Court reverses it later, like the Court did in the 1966 poll-tax case.

Lower courts, Congress, and the President are bound by the Supreme Court's rulings on the Constitution and interpretation of statutes and regulations.

If Congress doesn't like the Supreme Court's interpretation of a statute, Congress could repeal the statute or pass a new one to get a different outcome.

Caseload and the Court's Yearly Terms

For the most part, the Supreme Court chooses whether to hear cases. People petition the Court to hear a case, and the Justices vote on the petition.

These days, the Supreme Court receives over 7,000–8,000 petitions each year and chooses to hear less than 200 of them. Thus, it's not likely that a case will be heard by the Supreme Court.

The Supreme Court has yearly terms that start on the first Monday of each October and last until late June or early July. The Justices meet at the Supreme Court Building in Washington, D.C.

Process for Supreme Court Review

People usually ask the Supreme Court to review another court's ruling by petitioning for what's called a **writ of certiorari**. If the Court "grants cert" (decides to hear the case), the parties on each side submit briefs.

Like the circuit courts of appeal, the Supreme Court decides some cases based only on the briefs. In other cases, the Supreme Court allows oral arguments, too.

The Justices vote on how to rule on cases. If at least 5 of the 9 Justices agree on how a case should be decided, there is a **majority opinion**. The majority's opinion is the Court's opinion. Often, one Justice will write the majority's opinion.

Justices who disagree with the majority might write a **dissenting opinion** ("dissent" for short), explaining why they disagree with the majority. A Justice might also write a **concurring opinion**, which reaches the same result as the majority but for a different reason.

The Court's opinions are published so that other courts, lawyers, and the public can read them. Supreme Court opinions are online at multiple places, including www.supremecourt.gov.

Specialty Courts & Judges

Congress has created specialty courts that have limited jurisdiction to handle specific types of cases. Below are a few examples of those courts:

- Court of International Trade.

- Foreign Intelligence Surveillance Court (FISA).

- Tax Court.

- Court of Appeals for the Armed Services.

- Court of Appeals for Veterans Claims.

Judges on those courts face different appointment processes and terms. For example, the President appoints judges to the Court of International Trade for life, with Senate approval. The Chief Justice of the Supreme Court appoints judges to the Foreign Intelligence Surveillance Court for 7-year terms.

Administrative Law Judges

As covered in Chapter 3, administrative law judges (ALJs) are a different breed. ALJs adjudicate disputes—similar to Judicial Branch judges—but ALJs **work for Executive Branch agencies.**

ALJs' decisions can be appealed, usually to an agency's appellate body. Eventually, a Judicial Branch court may review an ALJ's decision. Different agencies have different procedures for handling appeals.

In the past, ALJs were hired under the competitive civil-service system, which required them to take exams. To promote ALJs' independence, the Administrative Procedures Act prevented them from being removed from office except for good cause.

In 2018, the U.S. Supreme Court ruled that ALJs (at least some) must be appointed by a president, a department head, or a court.[4] The Court's holding may or may not diminish ALJs' independence in the long run.

Judicial Branch Agencies

The Judicial Branch has a few agencies, including—

- The Administrative Offices of the U.S. Courts.
- The U.S. Sentencing Commission.
- The Supreme Court Police.

The **Administrative Offices** support federal courts by providing legislative, technological, management, and budget-related services. The **Sentencing Commission** reports on criminal-sentencing practices and makes recommendations about those practices. The **Supreme Court Police** protect the Justices, the building, and people in the building.

---

[4]   *Lucia v. S.E.C.*, 138 S. Ct. 2044, 2051 and 2055 (2018).

Text of the United States Constitution

The document text below is from the National Archives' transcript of the U.S. Constitution. It's the original text, as you can tell from the old-style spelling, phrasing, and punctuation.

The Constitution doesn't have descriptive headings. I added headings and bolded some text to make it easier for you to find things. I also added a few explanations and other words. Any added words are between **brackets** that look like this: [ ]

The Document's Text

[Preamble]

We the People of the United States, in Order to form a more perfect Union, establish Justice, insure domestic Tranquility, provide for the common defence, promote the general Welfare, and secure the Blessings of Liberty to ourselves and our Posterity, **do ordain and establish this Constitution** for the United States of America.

Article I

[Congress]

Section 1.

All **legislative Powers** herein granted shall be vested in a **Congress** of the United States, which shall consist of a Senate and House of Representatives.

Section 2.

The **House of Representatives** shall be composed of Members **chosen every second Year** by the People of the several States, and the Electors in each State shall have the Qualifications requisite for Electors of the most numerous Branch of the State Legislature.

No Person shall be a Representative who shall not have attained to the **Age of twenty five** Years, and been s**even Years a Citizen** of the United States, and who shall not, when elected, be an **Inhabitant of that State** in which he shall be chosen.

Representatives and direct Taxes shall be apportioned among the several States which may be included within this Union, according to their respective Numbers, which shall be determined by adding to the whole Number of free Persons, including those bound to Service for a Term of Years, and excluding Indians not taxed, three fifths of all other Persons.

[The italicized text was replaced or affected by 14th and 16th Amendments].

The actual Enumeration shall be made within three Years after the first Meeting of the Congress of the United States, and within every subsequent Term of ten Years, in such Manner as they shall by Law direct. The Number of Representatives shall not exceed one for every thirty Thousand, but each State shall have at Least one Representative; **and until such enumeration shall be made**, *the State of New Hampshire shall be entitled to chuse three, Massachusetts eight, Rhode-Island and Providence Plantations one, Connecticut five, New-York six, New Jersey four, Pennsylvania eight, Delaware one, Maryland six, Virginia ten, North Carolina five, South Carolina five, and Georgia three.*

[About the italicized text in the preceding paragraph: the number of representatives for each state has changed.]

When **vacancies** happen in the Representation from any State, the Executive Authority thereof shall issue Writs of Election to fill such Vacancies.

The House of Representatives shall chuse their **Speaker** and other Officers; and shall have the sole **Power of Impeachment.**

Section 3.

The Senate of the United States shall be composed of two Senators from each State, *chosen by the Legislature thereof*, for **six Years;** and each Senator shall have one Vote.

[The italicized text in the preceding paragraph was affected or replaced by the 17th Amendment: senators are now elected by the people.]

Immediately after they shall be assembled in Consequence of the first Election, they shall be divided as equally as may be into three Classes. The Seats of the **Senators of the first Class** shall be vacated at the Expiration of the second Year, of the **second Class** at the Expiration of the fourth Year, and of the **third Class** at the Expiration of the sixth Year, so that one third may be chosen every second Year; *and if Vacancies happen by Resignation, or otherwise, during the Recess of the Legislature of any State, the Executive thereof may make temporary Appointments until the next Meeting of the Legislature, which shall then fill such Vacancies.*

> [The italicized text in the preceding paragraph was replaced or affected by the 17th Amendment.]

No Person shall be a Senator who shall not have attained to the **Age of thirty Years**, and been **nine Years a Citizen** of the United States, and who shall not, when elected, be an **Inhabitant of that State** for which he shall be chosen.

The **Vice President** of the United States shall be **President of the Senate**, but shall have no Vote, unless they be equally divided.

The Senate shall chuse their other Officers, and also a **President pro tempore**, in the Absence of the Vice President, or when he shall exercise the Office of President of the United States.

The **Senate shall have the sole Power to try all Impeachments**. When sitting for that Purpose, they shall be on Oath or Affirmation. When the President of the United States is tried, the Chief Justice shall preside: And no Person shall be convicted without the Concurrence of two thirds of the Members present.

Judgment in Cases of **Impeachment** shall not extend further than to removal from Office, and disqualification to hold and enjoy any Office of honor, Trust or Profit under the United States: but the Party convicted shall nevertheless be liable and subject to Indictment, Trial, Judgment and Punishment, according to Law.

Section 4.

The **Times, Places and Manner of holding Elections** for Senators and Representatives, shall be prescribed in each State by the Legislature thereof; but the Congress may at any time by Law make or alter such Regulations, except as to the Places of chusing Senators.

The **Congress shall assemble** at least once in every Year, and such Meeting shall be *on the first Monday in December*, unless they shall by Law appoint a different Day.

[The italicized text in the preceding paragraph was replaced or affected by 20th Amendment.]

Section 5.

Each House shall be the Judge of the **Elections, Returns and Qualifications** of its own Members, and a Majority of each shall constitute a Quorum to do Business; but a smaller Number may adjourn from day to day, and may be authorized to compel the Attendance of absent Members, in such Manner, and under such Penalties as each House may provide.

Each House may determine the **Rules of its Proceeding**s, punish its Members for disorderly Behaviour, and, with the Concurrence of two thirds, expel a Member.

Each House shall keep a **Journal of its Proceedings**, and from time to time publish the same, excepting such Parts as may in their Judgment require Secrecy; and the Yeas and Nays of the Members of either House on any question shall, at the Desire of one fifth of those Present, be entered on the Journal.

Neither House, during the Session of Congress, shall, without the Consent of the other, **adjourn** for more than three days, nor to any other Place than that in which the two Houses shall be sitting.

Section 6.

The Senators and Representatives shall receive a **Compensation** for their Services, to be ascertained by Law, and paid out of the Treasury of the United States. They shall in all Cases, except Treason, Felony and Breach of the Peace, be **privileged from Arrest** during their Attendance at the Session of their respective Houses, and in going to and returning from the same; and for any Speech or Debate in either House, they shall not be questioned in any other Place.

No Senator or Representative shall, during the Time for which he was elected, be appointed to any civil Office under the Authority of the United States, which shall have been created, or the Emoluments whereof shall have been encreased during such time; and no Person holding any Office under the United States, shall be a Member of either House during his Continuance in Office.

Section 7.

All **Bills for raising Revenue** shall originate in the House of Representatives; but the Senate may propose or concur with Amendments as on other Bills.

Every **Bill** which shall have passed the House of Representatives and the Senate, shall, before it become a Law, be **presented to the President** of the United States; If he approve he shall sign it, but if not he shall return it, with his Objections to that House in which it shall have originated, who shall enter the Objections at large on their Journal, and proceed to reconsider it. If after such Reconsideration two thirds of that House shall agree to pass the Bill, it shall be sent, together with the Objections, to the other House, by which it shall likewise be reconsidered, and if approved by two thirds of that House, it shall become a Law. But in all such Cases the Votes of both Houses shall be determined by yeas and Nays, and the Names of the Persons voting for and against the Bill shall be entered on the **Journal** of each House respectively. If any Bill shall not be returned by the President within ten Days (Sundays excepted) after it shall have been presented to him, the Same shall be a Law, in like Manner as if he had signed it, unless the Congress by their Adjournment prevent its Return, in which Case it shall not be a Law.

Every Order, Resolution, or Vote to which the Concurrence of the Senate and House of Representatives may be necessary (except on a question of Adjournment) shall be presented to the President of the United States; and before the Same shall take Effect, shall be approved by him, or being disapproved by him, shall be repassed by two thirds of the Senate and House of Representatives, according to the Rules and Limitations prescribed in the Case of a Bill.

Section 8. [Enumerated powers of Congress]

The **Congress shall have Power** To lay and collect **Taxes, Duties, Imposts and Excises**, to **pay the Debts** and provide for the **common Defence** and **general Welfare** of the United States; but all Duties, Imposts and Excises shall be uniform throughout the United States;

To **borrow Money** on the credit of the United States;

To **regulate Commerce** with foreign Nations, and among the several States, and with the Indian Tribes;

To establish an uniform Rule of **Naturalization**, and uniform Laws on the subject of **Bankruptcies** throughout the United States;

To **coin Money**, regulate the Value thereof, and of foreign Coin, and fix the Standard of **Weights and Measures**;

To provide for the Punishment of counterfeiting the Securities and current Coin of the United States;

To establish **Post Offices** and post Roads;

To promote the Progress of **Science and useful Arts**, by securing for limited Times to Authors and Inventors the exclusive Right to their respective Writings and Discoveries;

To **constitute Tribunals** inferior to the supreme Court;

To define and punish **Piracies and Felonies committed on the high Seas**, and Offences against the Law of Nations;

To **declare War**, grant Letters of Marque and Reprisal, and make Rules concerning Captures on Land and Water;

To **raise and support Armies**, but no Appropriation of Money to that Use shall be for a longer Term than two Years;

To provide and maintain a **Navy**;

To make Rules for the Government and Regulation of the **land and naval Forces**;

To provide for calling forth the Militia to execute the Laws of the Union, **suppress Insurrections and repel Invasions**;

To provide for **organizing, arming, and disciplining, the Militia**, and for governing such Part of them as may be employed in the Service of the United States, reserving to the States respectively, the Appointment of the Officers, and the Authority of training the Militia according to the discipline prescribed by Congress;

To exercise exclusive Legislation in all Cases whatsoever, over such District (not exceeding ten Miles square) as may, by Cession of particular States, and the Acceptance of Congress, become the **Seat of the Government of the United States**, and to exercise like Authority over all Places purchased by the Consent of the Legislature of the State in which the Same shall be, for the Erection of Forts, Magazines, Arsenals, dock-Yards, and other needful Buildings;—And

To make all **Laws which shall be necessary and proper** for carrying into Execution the foregoing Powers, and all other Powers vested by this Constitution in the Government of the United States, or in any Department or Officer thereof.

Section 9.

The **Migration or Importation of such Persons** as any of the States now existing shall think proper to admit, shall not be prohibited by the Congress prior to the Year one thousand eight hundred and eight, but a Tax or duty may be imposed on such Importation, not exceeding ten dollars for each Person.

The Privilege of the **Writ of Habeas Corpus** shall not be suspended, unless when in Cases of Rebellion or Invasion the public Safety may require it.

No **Bill of Attainder** or **ex post facto Law** shall be passed.

No Capitation, or other direct, Tax shall be laid, *unless in Proportion to the Census or enumeration herein before directed to be taken.*

[The italicized text in the preceding paragraph was replaced or affected by the 16th Amendment.]

No Tax or Duty shall be laid on Articles exported from any State.

No Preference shall be given by any **Regulation of Commerce or Revenue to the Ports** of one State over those of another: nor shall Vessels bound to, or from, one State, be obliged to enter, clear, or pay Duties in another.

No **Money shall be drawn from the Treasury**, but in Consequence of Appropriations made by Law; and a regular Statement and Account of the Receipts and Expenditures of all public Money shall be published from time to time.

No Title of Nobility shall be granted by the United States: And no Person holding any Office of Profit or Trust under them, shall, without the Consent of the Congress, accept of any present,

Emolument, Office, or Title, of any kind whatever, from any King, Prince, or foreign State.

Section 10.

No State shall enter into any **Treaty**, Alliance, or Confederation; grant Letters of Marque and Reprisal; **coin Money**; emit Bills of Credit; make any Thing but gold and silver Coin a Tender in Payment of Debts; pass any **Bill of Attainder**, **ex post facto Law**, or Law impairing the Obligation of Contracts, or grant any **Title of Nobility**.

No State shall, without the Consent of the Congress, lay any **Imposts or Duties** on Imports or Exports, except what may be absolutely necessary for executing it's inspection Laws: and the net Produce of all Duties and Imposts, laid by any State on Imports or Exports, shall be for the Use of the Treasury of the United States; and all such Laws shall be subject to the Revision and Controul of the Congress.

No State shall, without the Consent of Congress, lay any Duty of Tonnage, keep Troops, or Ships of War in time of Peace, enter into any Agreement or Compact with another State, or with a foreign Power, or engage in War, unless actually invaded, or in such imminent Danger as will not admit of delay.

Article II

[Executive Branch: President, Vice President, etc.]

Section 1.

The **executive Power shall be vested in a President** of the United States of America. He shall hold his Office during the **Term of four Years**, and, together with the **Vice President**, chosen for the same Term, be elected, as follows

Each State shall appoint, in such Manner as the Legislature thereof may direct, a Number of Electors, equal to the whole Number of Senators and Representatives to which the State may be entitled in the Congress: but no Senator or Representative, or Person holding an Office of Trust or Profit under the United States, shall be appointed an Elector.

The Electors shall meet in their respective States, and vote by Ballot for two Persons, of whom one at least shall not be an Inhabitant of the same State with themselves. And they shall make a List of all the Persons voted for, and of the Number of Votes for each; which List they shall sign and certify, and transmit sealed to the Seat of the Government of the United States, directed to the President of the Senate. The President of the Senate shall, in the Presence of the Senate and House of Representatives, open all the Certificates, and the Votes shall then be counted. The Person having the greatest Number of Votes shall be the President, if such Number be a Majority of the whole Number of Electors appointed; and if there be more than one who have such Majority, and have an equal Number of Votes, then the House of Representatives shall immediately chuse by Ballot one of them for President; and if no Person have a Majority, then from the five highest on the List the said House shall in like Manner chuse the President. But in chusing the President, the Votes shall be taken by States, the Representation from each State having one Vote; A quorum for this Purpose shall consist of a Member or Members from two thirds of the States, and a Majority of all the States shall be necessary to a Choice. In every Case, after the Choice of the President, the Person having the greatest Number of Votes of the Electors shall be the Vice President. But if there should remain two or more who have equal Votes, the Senate shall chuse from them by Ballot the Vice President.

[The italicized text in the preceding paragraph was replaced or affected by 12th Amendment.]

The Congress may determine the Time of chusing the Electors, and the **Day on which they shall give their Votes**; which Day shall be the same throughout the United States.

No Person except a **natural born Citizen**, or a Citizen of the United States, at the time of the Adoption of this Constitution, shall be eligible to the Office of President; neither shall any Person be eligible to that Office who shall not have attained to the **Age of thirty five Years**, and been **fourteen Years a Resident** within the United States.

In Case of the Removal of the President from Office, or of his Death, Resignation, or Inability to discharge the Powers and Duties of the said Office, the Same shall devolve on the Vice President, and the Congress may by Law provide for the Case of Removal, Death, Resignation or Inability, both of the President and Vice President, declaring what Officer shall then act as President, and such Officer shall act accordingly, until the Disability be removed, or a President shall be elected.

[The italicized text in the preceding paragraph was replaced or affected by the 20th and 25th Amendments.]

The President shall, at stated Times, receive for his Services, a **Compensation**, which shall neither be encreased nor diminished during the Period for which he shall have been elected, and he shall not receive within that Period any other Emolument from the United States, or any of them.

Before he enter on the Execution of his Office, he shall take the following **Oath** or Affirmation:—"I do solemnly swear (or affirm) that I will faithfully execute the Office of President of the United States, and will to the best of my Ability, preserve, protect and defend the Constitution of the United States."

Section 2.

The President shall be **Commander in Chief** of the Army and Navy of the United States, and of the Militia of the several States, when called into the actual Service of the United States; he may require the Opinion, in writing, of the principal Officer in each of the executive Departments, upon any Subject relating to the Duties of their respective Offices, and he shall have Power to grant Reprieves and **Pardons** for Offences against the United States, except in Cases of Impeachment.

He shall have Power, by and with the Advice and Consent of the Senate, to make **Treaties**, provided two thirds of the Senators present concur; and he shall nominate, and by and with the Advice and Consent of the Senate, shall appoint **Ambassadors**, other public Ministers and Consuls, **Judges** of the supreme Court, and all **other Officers** of the United States, whose Appointments are not herein otherwise provided for, and which shall be established by Law: but the Congress may by Law vest the Appointment of such inferior Officers, as they think proper, in the President alone, in the Courts of Law, or in the Heads of Departments.

The President shall have Power to **fill up all Vacancies** that may happen during the Recess of the Senate, by granting Commissions which shall expire at the End of their next Session.

Section 3.

He shall from time to time give to the Congress Information of the **State of the Union**, and recommend to their Consideration such Measures as he shall judge necessary and expedient; he may, on extraordinary Occasions, **convene both Houses**, or either of them, and in Case of Disagreement between them, with Respect to the Time of Adjournment, he may adjourn them to such Time as he shall think proper; he shall receive Ambassadors and other public

Ministers; he shall **take Care that the Laws be faithfully executed,** and shall Commission all the Officers of the United States.

Section 4.

The President, Vice President and all civil Officers of the United States, shall be **removed from Office** on Impeachment for, and Conviction of, Treason, Bribery, or other high Crimes and Misdemeanors.

Article III

[Judicial Branch]

Section 1.

The judicial Power of the United States, shall be vested in one **supreme Court**, and in such **inferior Courts** as the Congress may from time to time ordain and establish.

The **Judges**, both of the supreme and inferior Courts, shall hold their Offices **during good Behaviour**, and shall, at stated Times, receive for their Services, a **Compensation**, which shall not be diminished during their Continuance in Office.

Section 2.

The **judicial Power shall extend to all Cases**, in Law and Equity, arising under this Constitution, the Laws of the United States, and Treaties made, or which shall be made, under their Authority;—to all Cases affecting Ambassadors, other public Ministers and Consuls;—to all Cases of admiralty and maritime Jurisdiction;—to Controversies to which the United States shall be a Party;—to Controversies between two or more States;—*between a State and Citizens of another State,*—between Citizens of different States,—between Citizens of the same State claiming Lands under Grants of different States, and between a State, or the Citizens thereof, and foreign States, Citizens or Subjects.

[The italicized text in the preceding paragraph was replaced or affected by the 11th Amendment.]

In all Cases affecting Ambassadors, other public Ministers and Consuls, and those in which a State shall be Party, the supreme Court shall have **original Jurisdiction**. In all the other Cases before mentioned, the supreme Court shall have **appellate Jurisdiction**, both as to Law and Fact, with such Exceptions, and under such Regulations as the Congress shall make.

The Trial of all Crimes, except in Cases of Impeachment, shall be by **Jury**; and such Trial shall be held in the State where the said Crimes shall have been committed; but when not committed within any State, the Trial shall be at such Place or Places as the Congress may by Law have directed.

Section 3.

Treason against the United States, shall consist only in levying War against them, or in adhering to their Enemies, giving them Aid and Comfort. No Person shall be convicted of Treason unless on the Testimony of two Witnesses to the same overt Act, or on Confession in open Court.

The Congress shall have Power to declare the **Punishment of Treason**, but no Attainder of Treason shall work Corruption of Blood, or Forfeiture except during the Life of the Person attainted.

Article IV

[Relations between states and their citizens]

Section 1.

Full Faith and Credit shall be given in each State to the public Acts, Records, and judicial Proceedings of every other State. And the Congress may by general Laws prescribe the Manner in which such Acts, Records and Proceedings shall be proved, and the Effect thereof.

Section 2.

The Citizens of each State shall be entitled to all **Privileges and Immunities** of Citizens in the several States.

A Person charged in any State with Treason, Felony, or other Crime, who shall flee from Justice, and be found in another State, shall on Demand of the executive Authority of the State from which he fled, be delivered up, to be removed to the State having Jurisdiction of the Crime.

No Person held to Service or Labour in one State, under the Laws thereof, escaping into another, shall, in Consequence of any Law or Regulation therein, be discharged from such Service or Labour, but shall be delivered up on Claim of the Party to whom such Service or Labour may be due.

> [The italicized text in the preceding paragraph was replaced or affected by the 13th Amendment.]

Section 3.

New States may be admitted by the Congress into this Union; but no new State shall be formed or erected within the Jurisdiction of any other State; nor any State be formed by the Junction of two or more States, or Parts of States, without the Consent of the Legislatures of the States concerned as well as of the Congress.

The Congress shall have Power to dispose of and make all needful Rules and Regulations respecting the **Territory or other Property** belonging to the United States; and nothing in this Constitution shall be so construed as to Prejudice any Claims of the United States, or of any particular State.

Section 4.

The United States shall guarantee to every State in this Union a **Republican Form of Government**, and shall **protect each of them against Invasion**; and on Application of the Legislature, or of the

Executive (when the Legislature cannot be convened), against **domestic Violence.**

Article V

[How to amend the Constitution]

The Congress, whenever two thirds of both Houses shall deem it necessary, shall **propose Amendments** to this Constitution, or, on the Application of the Legislatures of two thirds of the several States, shall call a **Convention** for proposing Amendments, which, in either Case, shall be valid to all Intents and Purposes, as Part of this Constitution, when **ratified** by the Legislatures of three fourths of the several States, or by Conventions in three fourths thereof, as the one or the other Mode of Ratification may be proposed by the Congress; Provided that no Amendment which may be made prior to the Year One thousand eight hundred and eight shall in any Manner affect the first and fourth Clauses in the Ninth Section of the first Article; and that no State, without its Consent, shall be deprived of its equal Suffrage in the Senate.

Article VI

[Prior debts, supremacy of U.S. law,
oaths of office, no religious tests]

All **Debts** contracted and Engagements entered into, before the Adoption of this Constitution, shall be as valid against the United States under this Constitution, as under the Confederation.

This Constitution, and the Laws of the United States which shall be made in Pursuance thereof; and all Treaties made, or which shall be made, under the Authority of the United States, shall be the **supreme Law of the Land**; and the Judges in every State shall be bound thereby, any Thing in the Constitution or Laws of any State to the Contrary notwithstanding.

The Senators and Representatives before mentioned, and the Members of the several State Legislatures, and all executive and judicial Officers, both of the United States and of the several States, shall be bound by **Oath** or Affirmation, to support this Constitution; but no religious Test shall ever be required as a Qualification to any Office or public Trust under the United States.

Article VII

[Ratification of the Constitution]

The Ratification of the Conventions of nine States, shall be sufficient for the Establishment of this Constitution between the States so ratifying the Same.

The Word, "the," being interlined between the seventh and eighth Lines of the first Page, The Word "Thirty" being partly written on an Erazure in the fifteenth Line of the first Page, The Words "is tried" being interlined between the thirty second and thirty third Lines of the first Page and the Word "the" being interlined between the forty third and forty fourth Lines of the second Page.

Attest William Jackson Secretary

done in Convention by the Unanimous Consent of the States present **the Seventeenth Day of September in the Year of our Lord one thousand seven hundred and Eighty seven** and of the Independance of the United States of America the Twelfth In witness whereof We have hereunto subscribed our Names,

[Signers' names omitted: check online]

Amendments to the Constitution

[Preamble omitted]

[**Bill of Rights** is first 10 Amendments, ratified in 1791]

Amendment I [1st]

Congress shall make no law respecting an establishment of **religion**, or prohibiting the free exercise thereof; or abridging the **freedom of speech**, or of **the press**; or the right of the people **peaceably to assemble**, and to **petition the Government** for a redress of grievances.

Amendment II [2nd]

A well regulated Militia, being necessary to the security of a free State, the right of the people to **keep and bear Arms**, shall not be infringed.

Amendment III [3rd]

No Soldier shall, in time of peace **be quartered** in any house, without the consent of the Owner, nor in time of war, but in a manner to be prescribed by law.

Amendment IV [4th]

The right of the people to be secure in their persons, houses, papers, and effects, against **unreasonable searches and seizures**, shall not be violated, and no **Warrants** shall issue, but upon probable cause, supported by Oath or affirmation, and particularly describing the place to be searched, and the persons or things to be seized.

Amendment V [5th]

No person shall be held to answer for a capital, or otherwise infamous **crime**, unless on a presentment or indictment of a **Grand Jury**, except in cases arising in the land or naval forces, or in the Militia, when in actual service in time of War or public danger; nor shall any person be subject for the same offence to be **twice put in jeopardy** of life or limb; nor shall be compelled in any criminal case to be **a witness against himself**, nor be deprived of life, liberty, or property, without **due process of law**; nor shall **private property** be taken for public use, without just compensation.

Amendment VI [6th]

In all **criminal prosecutions**, the accused shall enjoy the right to a **speedy and public trial**, by an **impartial jury** of the State and district wherein the crime shall have been committed, which district shall have been previously ascertained by law, and to be informed of the nature and cause of the accusation; to be **confronted with the witnesses** against him; to have **compulsory process for obtaining witnesses** in his favor, and to have the **Assistance of Counsel** for his defence.

Amendment VII [7th]

In **Suits at common law**, where the value in controversy shall exceed twenty dollars, the right of **trial by jury** shall be preserved, and no fact tried by a jury, shall be otherwise re-examined in any Court of the United States, than according to the rules of the common law.

Amendment VIII [8th]

Excessive **bail** shall not be required, nor excessive **fines** imposed, nor **cruel and unusual punishments** inflicted.

Amendment IX [9th]

The enumeration in the Constitution, of certain rights, shall not be construed to deny or disparage others retained by the people.

Amendment X [10th]

The **powers** not delegated to the United States by the Constitution, nor prohibited by it to the States, are **reserved to the States** respectively, or to the people.

Other Amendments

Amendment XI [11th, ratified 1795]

The Judicial power of the United States shall not be construed to extend to any suit in law or equity, commenced or prosecuted against one of the United States by Citizens of another State, or by Citizens or Subjects of any Foreign State.

Amendment XII [12th, ratified 1804]

The Electors shall meet in their respective states and vote by **ballot for President and Vice-President,** one of whom, at least, shall not be an inhabitant of the same state with themselves; they shall name in their ballots the person voted for as President, and in distinct ballots the person voted for as Vice-President, and they shall make distinct lists of all persons voted for as President, and of all persons voted for as Vice-President, and of the number of votes for each, which lists they shall sign and certify, and transmit sealed to the seat of the government of the United States, directed to the President of the Senate;—the President of the Senate shall, in the presence of the Senate and House of Representatives, open all the certificates and the votes shall then be counted;—The person having the greatest number of votes for President, shall be the President, if such number be a majority of the whole number of Electors appointed; and if no person have such majority, then from the persons having the highest numbers not exceeding three on the list of those voted for as President, the House of Representatives shall choose immediately, by ballot, the President. But in choosing the President, the votes shall be taken by states, the representation from each state having one vote; a quorum for this purpose shall consist of a member or members from two-thirds of the states, and a majority of all the states shall be necessary to a choice. *And if the House of Representatives shall not choose a President whenever the right of choice shall devolve upon them, before the fourth day of March next following, then the Vice-President shall act as*

President, as in case of the death or other constitutional disability of the President.—The person having the greatest number of votes as Vice-President, shall be the Vice-President, if such number be a majority of the whole number of Electors appointed, and if no person have a majority, then from the two highest numbers on the list, the Senate shall choose the Vice-President; a quorum for the purpose shall consist of two-thirds of the whole number of Senators, and a majority of the whole number shall be necessary to a choice. But no person constitutionally ineligible to the office of President shall be eligible to that of Vice-President of the United States.

[The italicized text in the preceding paragraph was replaced or affected by 20th Amendment.]

Amendment XIII [13th, ratified 1865]

Section 1. Neither **slavery** nor involuntary servitude, except as a punishment for crime whereof the party shall have been duly convicted, shall exist within the United States, or any place subject to their jurisdiction.

Section 2. Congress shall have power to enforce this article by appropriate legislation.

Amendment XIV [14th, ratified in 1868]

Section 1. All persons born or naturalized in the United States, and subject to the jurisdiction thereof, are citizens of the United States and of the State wherein they reside. No State shall make or enforce any law which shall abridge the **privileges or immunities of citizens** of the United States; nor shall any State deprive any person of life, liberty, or property, without **due process of law**; nor deny to any person within its jurisdiction the **equal protection** of the laws.

Section 2. Representatives shall be apportioned among the several States according to their respective numbers, counting the whole number of persons in each State, excluding Indians not taxed.

But when the **right to vote** at any election for the choice of electors for President and Vice-President of the United States, Representatives in Congress, the Executive and Judicial officers of a State, or the members of the Legislature thereof, is denied to any of the **male** inhabitants of such State, *being twenty-one years of age*, and citizens of the United States, or in any way abridged, except for participation in rebellion, or other crime, the basis of representation therein shall be reduced in the proportion which the number of such male citizens shall bear to the whole number of male citizens twenty-one years of age in such State.

[The italicized text in the preceding paragraph was replaced or affected by 26th Amendment.]

Section 3. No person shall be a Senator or Representative in Congress, or elector of President and Vice-President, or hold any office, civil or military, under the United States, or under any State, who, having previously taken an oath, as a member of Congress, or as an officer of the United States, or as a member of any State legislature, or as an executive or judicial officer of any State, to support the Constitution of the United States, shall have engaged in insurrection or rebellion against the same, or given aid or comfort to the enemies thereof. But Congress may by a vote of two-thirds of each House, remove such disability.

Section 4. The validity of the **public debt** of the United States, authorized by law, including debts incurred for payment of pensions and bounties for services in suppressing insurrection or rebellion, shall not be questioned. But neither the United States nor any State shall assume or pay any debt or obligation incurred in aid of insurrection or rebellion against the United States, or any claim for the loss or emancipation of any slave; but all such debts, obligations and claims shall be held illegal and void.

Section 5. The Congress shall have the **power to enforce**, by appropriate legislation, the provisions of this article.

Amendment XV [15th, ratified 1870]

Section 1. The right of citizens of the United States to **vote** shall not be denied or abridged by the United States or by any State on account of **race, color,** or previous condition of servitude—

Section 2. The Congress shall have the **power to enforce** this article by appropriate legislation.

Amendment XVI [16th, ratified 1913]

The Congress shall have power to lay and collect **taxes on incomes,** from whatever source derived, without apportionment among the several States, and without regard to any census or enumeration.

Amendment XVII [17th, ratified 1913]

The Senate of the United States shall be composed of two **Senators** from each State, **elected by the people** thereof, for six years; and each Senator shall have one vote. The electors in each State shall have the qualifications requisite for electors of the most numerous branch of the State legislatures.

When **vacancies** happen in the representation of any State **in the Senate**, the executive authority of such State shall issue writs of election to fill such vacancies: Provided, That the legislature of any State may empower the executive thereof to make temporary appointments until the people fill the vacancies by election as the legislature may direct.

This amendment shall not be so construed as to affect the election or term of any Senator chosen before it becomes valid as part of the Constitution

Amendment XVIII [18th, ratified 1919]

Section 1. After one year from the ratification of this article the manufacture, sale, or transportation of **intoxicating liquors** within, the importation thereof into, or the exportation thereof from the

United States and all territory subject to the jurisdiction thereof for beverage purposes is hereby prohibited.

Section 2. The Congress and the several States shall have concurrent power to enforce this article by appropriate legislation.

Section 3. This article shall be inoperative unless it shall have been ratified as an amendment to the Constitution by the legislatures of the several States, as provided in the Constitution, within seven years from the date of the submission hereof to the States by the Congress.

[The 18th Amendment was repealed by the 21st Amendment.]

Amendment XIX [19th, ratified 1920]

The right of citizens of the United States to **vote** shall not be denied or abridged by the United States or by any State on account of **sex.**

Congress shall have **power to enforce** this article by appropriate legislation.

Amendment XX [20th, ratified 1933]

Section 1. The **terms** of the President and the Vice President shall end at noon on the 20th day of January, and the terms of Senators and Representatives at noon on the 3d day of January, of the years in which such terms would have ended if this article had not been ratified; and the terms of their successors shall then begin.

Section 2. The **Congress shall assemble** at least once in every year, and such meeting shall begin at noon on the 3d day of January, unless they shall by law appoint a different day.

Section 3. If, at the time fixed for the beginning of the term of the President, **the President elect shall have died**, the Vice President elect shall become President. If a President shall not have been chosen before the time fixed for the beginning of his term, or if the President elect shall have failed to qualify, then the Vice

President elect shall act as President until a President shall have qualified; and the Congress may by law provide for the case wherein neither a President elect nor a Vice President elect shall have qualified, declaring who shall then act as President, or the manner in which one who is to act shall be selected, and such person shall act accordingly until a President or Vice President shall have qualified.

Section 4. The Congress may by law provide for the case of the death of any of the persons from whom the House of Representatives may choose a President whenever the right of choice shall have devolved upon them, and for the case of the death of any of the persons from whom the Senate may choose a Vice President whenever the right of choice shall have devolved upon them.

Section 5. Sections 1 and 2 shall take effect on the 15th day of October following the ratification of this article.

Section 6. This article shall be inoperative unless it shall have been ratified as an amendment to the Constitution by the legislatures of three-fourths of the several States within seven years from the date of its submission.

Amendment XXI [21st, ratified 1933]

Section 1. The **eighteenth** article of **amendment** to the Constitution of the United States is hereby **repealed**.

Section 2. The transportation or importation into any State, Territory, or possession of the United States for delivery or use therein of **intoxicating liquors**, in violation of the laws thereof, is hereby prohibited.

Section 3. This article shall be inoperative unless it shall have been ratified as an amendment to the Constitution by conventions in the several States, as provided in the Constitution, within seven years from the date of the submission hereof to the States by the Congress.

Amendment XXII [22nd, ratified 1951]

Section 1. No person shall be **elected to the office of the President more than twice**, and no person who has held the office of President, or acted as President, for more than two years of a term to which some other person was elected President shall be elected to the office of the President more than once. But this Article shall not apply to any person holding the office of President when this Article was proposed by the Congress, and shall not prevent any person who may be holding the office of President, or acting as President, during the term within which this Article becomes operative from holding the office of President or acting as President during the remainder of such term.

Section 2. This article shall be inoperative unless it shall have been ratified as an amendment to the Constitution by the legislatures of three-fourths of the several States within seven years from the date of its submission to the States by the Congress.

Amendment XXIII [23rd, ratified 1961]

Section 1. The **District** [Washington D.C.] constituting the seat of Government of the United States shall appoint in such manner as the Congress may direct: A number of **electors of President and Vice President** equal to the whole number of Senators and Representatives in Congress to which the District would be entitled if it were a State, but in no event more than the least populous State; they shall be in addition to those appointed by the States, but they shall be considered, for the purposes of the election of President and Vice President, to be electors appointed by a State; and they shall meet in the District and perform such duties as provided by the twelfth article of amendment.

Section 2. The Congress shall have **power to enforce** this article by appropriate legislation.

Amendment XXIV [24th, ratified 1964]

Section 1. The **right** of citizens of the United States **to vote** in any primary or other election for President or Vice President, for electors for President or Vice President, or for Senator or Representative in Congress, shall not be denied or abridged by the United States or any State by reason of failure to pay any **poll tax** or other tax.

Section 2. The Congress shall have **power to enforce** this article by appropriate legislation.

Amendment XXV [25th, ratified 1967]

Section 1. In case of the **removal of the President** from office or of his death or resignation, the Vice President shall become President.

Section 2. Whenever there is a **vacancy in the office of the Vice President**, the President shall nominate a Vice President who shall take office upon confirmation by a majority vote of both Houses of Congress.

Section 3. Whenever the **President** transmits to the President pro tempore of the Senate and the Speaker of the House of Representatives his written declaration that he is **unable to discharge the powers and duties** of his office, and until he transmits to them a written declaration to the contrary, such powers and duties shall be discharged by the Vice President as Acting President.

Section 4. Whenever the **Vice President and a majority of either the principal officers** of the executive departments or of such other body as Congress may by law provide, transmit to the President pro tempore of the Senate and the Speaker of the House of

Representatives their written declaration that the **President is unable** to discharge the powers and duties of his office, the Vice President shall immediately assume the powers and duties of the office as Acting President.

Thereafter, when the **President** transmits to the President pro tempore of the Senate and the Speaker of the House of Representatives his written declaration that no inability exists, he shall **resume the powers and duties** of his office unless the Vice President and a majority of either the principal officers of the executive department or of such other body as Congress may by law provide, transmit within four days to the President pro tempore of the Senate and the Speaker of the House of Representatives their written declaration that the President is unable to discharge the powers and duties of his office. Thereupon Congress shall decide the issue, assembling within forty-eight hours for that purpose if not in session. If the Congress, within twenty-one days after receipt of the latter written declaration, or, if Congress is not in session, within twenty-one days after Congress is required to assemble, determines by two-thirds vote of both Houses that the President is unable to discharge the powers and duties of his office, the Vice President shall continue to discharge the same as Acting President; otherwise, the President shall resume the powers and duties of his office.

Amendment XXVI [26th, ratified 1971]

Section 1. The right of citizens of the United States, who are **eighteen years of age** or older, to **vote** shall not be denied or abridged by the United States or by any State on account of age.

Section 2. The Congress shall have **power to enforce** this article by appropriate legislation.

Amendment XXVII [27th, ratified 1992]

No law, varying the **compensation** for the services of the **Senators** and **Representatives**, shall take effect, until an election of Representatives shall have intervened.

Annotated and Reformatted Text of *Declaration of Independence*

The text (from the National Archives, www.archives.gov) is original and has not been altered. The punctuation and spelling were left intact, the rules of which were different 200+ years ago.

Paragraph breaks, bolding, italicizing, and headings were inserted to make the text easier to read.

In Congress, July 4, 1776.

[People's & Government's Rights, Powers and Duties]

The unanimous Declaration of the thirteen united States of America, When in the Course of human events, it becomes necessary for one people to dissolve the political bands which have connected them with another, and to assume among the powers of the earth, the separate and equal station to which the Laws of Nature and of

Nature's God entitle them, a decent respect to the opinions of mankind requires that they should declare the causes which impel them to the separation.

We hold these truths to be self-evident, that all men are created equal, that they are endowed by their Creator with certain unalienable Rights, that among these are Life, Liberty and the pursuit of Happiness.

—That to secure these rights, Governments are instituted among Men, deriving their just powers from the consent of the governed,

—That whenever any Form of Government becomes destructive of these ends, it is the Right of the People to alter or to abolish it, and to institute new Government, laying its foundation on such principles and organizing its powers in such form, as to them shall seem most likely to effect their Safety and Happiness.

Prudence, indeed, will dictate that Governments long established should not be changed for light and transient causes; and accordingly all experience hath shewn, that mankind are more disposed to suffer, while evils are sufferable, than to right themselves by abolishing the forms to which they are accustomed.

But when a long train of abuses and usurpations, pursuing invariably the same Object evinces a design to reduce them under absolute Despotism, it is their right, it is their duty, to throw off such Government, and to provide new Guards for their future security.

[British King's Tyranny & Abuse of Power]

—Such has been the patient sufferance of these Colonies; and such is now the necessity which constrains them to alter their former Systems of Government.

The history of the present King of Great Britain is a history of repeated injuries and usurpations, all having in direct object the establishment of an absolute Tyranny over these States. To prove this, let Facts be submitted to a candid world.

He has refused his Assent to Laws, the most wholesome and necessary for the public good.

He has forbidden his Governors to pass Laws of immediate and pressing importance, unless suspended in their operation till his Assent should be obtained; and when so suspended, he has utterly neglected to attend to them.

He has refused to pass other Laws for the accommodation of large districts of people, unless those people would relinquish the right of Representation in the Legislature, a right inestimable to them and formidable to tyrants only.

He has called together legislative bodies at places unusual, uncomfortable, and distant from the depository of their public Records, for the sole purpose of fatiguing them into compliance with his measures.

He has dissolved Representative Houses repeatedly, for opposing with manly firmness his invasions on the rights of the people.

He has refused for a long time, after such dissolutions, to cause others to be elected; whereby the Legislative powers, incapable of Annihilation, have returned to the People at large for their exercise; the State remaining in the mean time exposed to all the dangers of invasion from without, and convulsions within.

He has endeavoured to prevent the population of these States; for that purpose obstructing the Laws for Naturalization of Foreigners; refusing to pass others to encourage their migrations hither, and raising the conditions of new Appropriations of Lands.

He has obstructed the Administration of Justice, by refusing his Assent to Laws for establishing Judiciary powers.

He has made Judges dependent on his Will alone, for the tenure of their offices, and the amount and payment of their salaries.

He has erected a multitude of New Offices, and sent hither swarms of Officers to harrass our people, and eat out their substance.

He has kept among us, in times of peace, Standing Armies without the Consent of our legislatures.

He has affected to render the Military independent of and superior to the Civil power.

He has combined with others to subject us to a jurisdiction foreign to our constitution, and unacknowledged by our laws; giving his Assent to their Acts of pretended Legislation:

For Quartering large bodies of armed troops among us:

For protecting them, by a mock Trial, from punishment for any Murders which they should commit on the Inhabitants of these States:

For cutting off our Trade with all parts of the world:

For imposing Taxes on us without our Consent:

For depriving us in many cases, of the benefits of Trial by Jury:

For transporting us beyond Seas to be tried for pretended offences

For abolishing the free System of English Laws in a neighbouring Province, establishing therein an Arbitrary government, and enlarging its Boundaries so as to render it at once an example and fit instrument for introducing the same absolute rule into these Colonies:

For taking away our Charters, abolishing our most valuable Laws, and altering fundamentally the Forms of our Governments:

For suspending our own Legislatures, and declaring themselves invested with power to legislate for us in all cases whatsoever.

He has abdicated Government here, by declaring us out of his Protection and waging War against us.

He has plundered our seas, ravaged our Coasts, burnt our towns, and destroyed the lives of our people.

He is at this time transporting large Armies of foreign Mercenaries to compleat the works of death, desolation and tyranny, already begun with circumstances of Cruelty & perfidy scarcely paralleled in the most barbarous ages, and totally unworthy the Head of a civilized nation.

He has constrained our fellow Citizens taken Captive on the high Seas to bear Arms against their Country, to become the executioners of their friends and Brethren, or to fall themselves by their Hands.

He has excited domestic insurrections amongst us, and has endeavoured to bring on the inhabitants of our frontiers, the merciless Indian Savages, whose known rule of warfare, is an undistinguished destruction of all ages, sexes and conditions.

In every stage of these Oppressions We have Petitioned for Redress in the most humble terms: Our repeated Petitions have been answered only by repeated injury.

A Prince whose character is thus marked by every act which may define a Tyrant, is unfit to be the ruler of a free people.

Nor have We been wanting in attentions to our Brittish brethren. We have warned them from time to time of attempts by their legislature to extend an unwarrantable jurisdiction over us. We have reminded them of the circumstances of our emigration and settlement here. We have appealed to their native justice and magnanimity, and we have conjured them by the ties of our common kindred to disavow these usurpations, which, would inevitably interrupt our connections and correspondence. They too have been deaf to the voice of justice and of consanguinity. We must, therefore, acquiesce in the necessity, which denounces our Separation, and hold them, as we hold the rest of mankind, Enemies in War, in Peace Friends.

[Declaration of Colonies' Intent to Become Independent from Britain]

We, therefore, the Representatives of the United States of America, in General Congress, Assembled, appealing to the Supreme Judge of the world for the rectitude of our intentions, do, in the Name, and by Authority of the good People of these Colonies, solemnly publish and declare, That these United Colonies are, and of Right ought to be Free and Independent States; that they are Absolved from all Allegiance to the British Crown, and that all political connection between them and the State of Great Britain, is and ought to be totally dissolved; and that as Free and Independent States, they have full Power to levy War, conclude Peace, contract Alliances, establish Commerce, and to do all other Acts and Things which Independent States may of right do. And for the support of this Declaration, with a firm reliance on the protection of divine Providence, we mutually pledge to each other our Lives, our Fortunes and our sacred Honor.